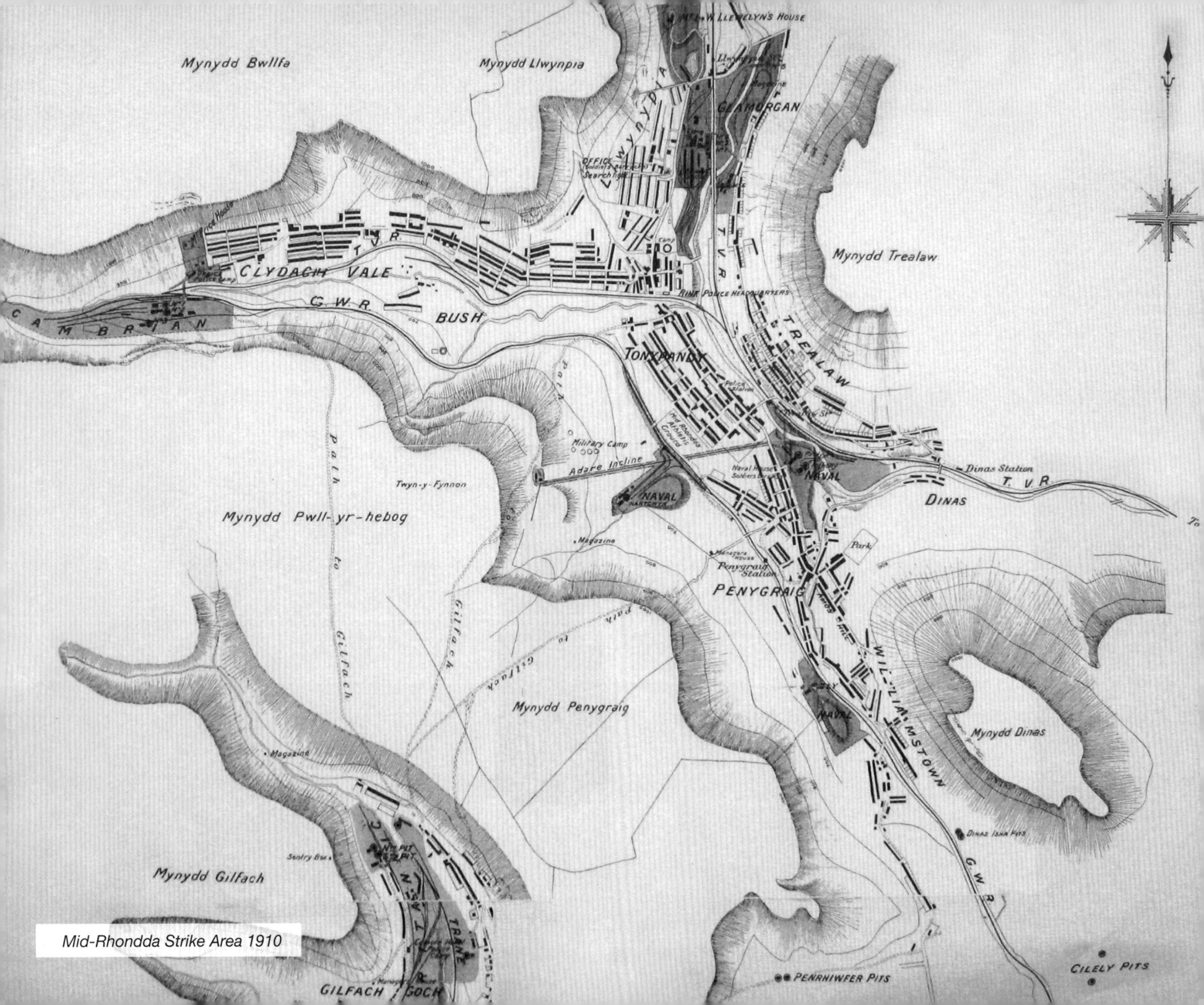
Mid-Rhondda Strike Area 1910

The Tonypandy Riots 1910-1911

Gwyn Evans
and David Maddox

The Authors

The material for this book emanated from a History and Art department project at Tonypandy Grammar school in the late 1960s and the early 70s. Interviews were recorded of people from the Mid-Rhondda community who had lived through the momentous events of the Cambrian Combine Strike 1910-11. Pupils undertook research into their families' history of the period. The work culminated in a school exhibition in 1974, which received a Prince of Wales Award and a British Petroleum Heritage Award. The exhibition was transferred to the National Museum of Wales, Cardiff, in 1975.

The authors published a booklet and slide set, 'The Tonypandy Riots' (Mid Glamorgan County Council 1992) and a resource pack for schools, 'The Cambrian Combine Strike' (Tonypandy Community College with Heritage Lottery Funding in 2010).

The *'eye witness'* accounts and documentary sources used remain unchanged from their original form to reflect the colour and style of the period.

The authors wish to express their gratitude to **Professor Dai Smith** for kindly writing the foreword but also for his stimulating writing on the subject.
Dr. Stuart Broomfield and **Fay Swain** for kindly reading the proofs and for help and guidance.
Nick Kelland for advice on photographic resources.

David Rees, Seer Design for excellent advice on presentation and to **David** and **Coral Westcott** for allowing access to their superb collection of postcards.

The Authors

David Maddox was Head of History and Economics at Tonypandy Grammar School and Mid-Rhondda Comprehensive school before appointment as County Adviser for History, Economics and Politics for Mid Glamorgan LEA. He retired as Deputy Chief Adviser at ESIS (Education Support and Improvement Service) for Bridgend, Caerphilly, Merthyr Tydfil and Rhondda Cynon Taf County Borough Councils.

He has been actively involved in producing Welsh history resources for schools for over 30 years. He is a former Chairman of the Association of History Teachers in Wales and a member of the Secretary of State for Wales' History Working Party for the National Curriculum. In recent years he has undertaken consultancies with BBC Education Wales, the Royal Commission for Ancient and Historical Monuments in Wales and Tinopolis. He has worked closely with Rhondda Cynon Taf's Tonypandy 1910-2010 Heritage Committee. He was awarded an OBE for services to education in Mid Glamorgan.

Gwyn Evans: Educated at Tonypandy Grammar School and Cardiff College of Art. After qualifying and completing National Service, he taught in schools in Coventry before taking up the post of Head of Art and Design at Tonypandy Grammar School and following reorganisation, at Tonypandy Comprehensive School until his retirement. A founder member of the Rhondda Group of painters he has exhibited with the Young Contemporaries, the Welsh Arts Council, Pictures for Schools and various group exhibitions. His work is held in both public and private collections.

First published: November 2010
ISBN: 978-1-84102-270-3
Published by University of Plymouth Press
Design: Seer Design. www.seerdesign.co.uk
Print: Zenith Media. www.zenith-media.co.uk
Copyright: © David Maddox and Gwyn Evans 2010

All rights reserved. No part of this publication may be produced, stored in a retrieval system or transmitted in any form or by any means, electronically, mechanical, photocopying, recording or otherwise, without permission of the copyright holders. The rights of David Maddox and Gwyn Evans, as the authors of this work, have been asserted by them in accordance with the copyright, Designs and Patents Act 1988.

The Acknowledgements

We are grateful to the staff of the following Libraries, Archival Services and Museum Services for their generous support:

Staff at Cardiff Central Library; Merthyr Tydfil County Borough Library (Carolyn Jacobs Reference Librarian); Public Record Office, London; Rhondda Cynon Taf Borough Council: (especially Nick Kelland Deputy Librarian); Pontypridd Library (Edwina Smart, Hywel Matthews reference librarian and Chris Radcliffe); Treorchy Reference Library (Anthony Pritchard); South Wales Miners' Library; Swansea University; Hendrefoilan; Glamorgan Record Office; Cardiff
The National Museum: Ceri Thompson, Curator Big Pit Mining Museum;
The Chief Constable, South Wales Constabulary: Police Museum, Bridgend (The late Ron Baker, formerly deputy Chief Constable of Glamorgan and Museum Archivist; PC Reg. Dodson formerly Curator Police Museum, Bridgend); Gareth Thomas, Chair South Wales Postcard Society

The following have been generous in allowing use of photographic and documentary material from their collections:

David and Coral Westcott 3, 5T, 5BR, 6BL, 9, 12TR, 15TR, 15 BR, 18BR, 18BL, 19TR, 25, 34, 35TL, 37, TL, 50BR, 54BL, 66, 79, 81, 82, 94, 108BL, 123TR, 147, 154.
The family of the late Cyril Batstone; 13TL, 13TR, 18TL, 27BR, 43, 60, 98, 134BR; David Carpenter; 14, 26TL, 110; Malcolm Coundley 101TL, 101TR; Gwyn Evans and David Maddox Photographic Collection Slides. 6BR, 8B, 11, 12TL, 12BL, 12BR, 16, 17, 20TL, 21, 22TR, 24, 31, 32, 35TR, 39, 41, 42, 46, 50BL, 52, 53, 55TR, 55BR, 59, 61, 62, 63, 63TR, 64, 65TL, 65BL, 67, 71, 72 BL, 97, 128TL, 73, 75, 77, 78TL, 78TR, 78B, 84, 91, 92, 99, 121, 122, 129, 133, 140BR, 143, 153 TR
Glamorgan Record Office, Cardiff 49, 68TL, 74TL, 74TR, 85, 111, 124TL, 142 TR

Beryl Goodwin, Llandaff 139 TL; Getty Images; 45, 47BR, 55L, 56, 57TL, 69, 80, 89, 135; Shirley James 8T; Emrys Jenkins 153BL; Media Wales 96TL, 96TR, 96BL, 108TL, 150, 159; Merthyr County Borough Library 139BL, 140TL, 142BR; National Museum of Wales; extracts from 'Coal Domain' by Dr.Bill Jones and Beth Thomas; National Museum of Wales 13 BR, 18TR, 29R, 40, 115, 131 National Museum Big Pit 117; Creighton Sims 137;
Rhondda Cynon Taf Borough Library 5BL, 6TL, 6TR, 20BR, 39TR, 106, 109, 123TL, 124TR, 124BL, 125, 127, 128TR, 134TL;
South Wales Police Museum 44, 104, 105, 113TL, 113BR, 126, 141, 142TL, 142BL, 144, Steven Rowson Collection 145; Valley Kids, Penygraig 15BL; Paul Young 22B, 23BL; Western Mail 29L,146; Gwernfil Williams 50TL, 118TR.

We are indebted to the following newspapers for allowing us to use selected press reports:

The Rhondda Leader, The Glamorgan Free Press, Pontypridd Observer, Glamorgan Gazette South Wales Echo and the Western Mail.
Grateful thanks is also given to Tina Davies and Matthew Robbins (ESIS) for clerical and reprographic support.

In memory of those who were prepared to share their invaluable stories of life during the troubled years 1910-11:

Thomas Bartlett
Thomas Morgan Bevan
Gwen Cunningham
Ben. R Davies
John Davies
Shaun Gordon
George Haines
Edith (nee Carpenter) Hancock
Harry Hobbs
Hywel Price James
Sarah Anne Jones
Annie Jones
William Henry Lewis (Bill 'Empire')
Phoebe Lloyd
W.J. Morris
Joseph Nutt
Albert Price
Arthur and Lilly Pontsford
Annie Stevens (Toms)
Annie Mary Thurston
Charles John Towells
John Wannell
Margaret Williams
George W. Richards

To our former pupils at Tonypandy Grammar school and their families:

Carol Baker — Helen Trotman
Dilun Fox — Janet Green
Gareth Hughes — Patrick Legge
Joanne Prior — David Roberts
Andrew Skinner — Simon Smith
Robert Stallard — Huw Thomas
Andrew Thomas — Philip Tuck
Lindsay Vickery

Foreword

"All that has been: All that is to come"

This book is full of remarkable photographs. None more so than that of the crowd assembled outside the Glamorgan Colliery on Monday, 7 November 1910. It is the still moment before the storm breaks. The cast is gathered on the set but the Director has not yet shouted "Lights! Camera! Action!" A thin cordon of police hem in the mass picket of striking miners at the gateway. Inside the Powerhouse, Leonard Llewellyn has grouped together his cohort of Glamorgan constabulary, soon to be stiffened in numbers and aggression by imported London Metropolitans. On the Wednesday the Army will arrive and stay as a crucial reserve for almost a year and so until the Cambrian Combine Strike is finally broken. But just for the moment on that cold Monday afternoon, Levi Ladd, the photographer from Tonypandy who was responsible for most of these images, has, from his vantage point on the embankment across the road, frozen the motion of the crowd. We see them, of course, as individual presences, but as a collective they have been formed by all that has gone before them in the rapid creation of the world's greatest concentration of Coal Capitalism in the pits of the Combine, and the attendant offshoots of housing, shops, schools, chapels, pubs and theatres that is their sudden and packed society. As individuals, they control neither their means to make a living nor the public life of the community in which they perforce live. Yet, as a collectivity, they are about to challenge those givens in the most direct fashion possible, and to become the most emblematic of the makers and shapers of twentieth century Wales.

Look now at the photograph of another mass assembly of the same strikers in the same place on the next day, Tuesday 8 November. It is the police who are here pushed to the limits of the picture,The crowd are no longer posing. Their backs are turned, indifferent to the effect of being "on camera". And the iron-stalked, glass-paned gas lamp to whose cross bars a man clings to be sure of being in the frame in the first photo is, in the second, twisted and shattered. That was the effect of fierce clashes with the police which came almost immediately after Ladd's portrait on Monday when the crowd was baton charged to stop their incessant stoning of the Powerhouse and the Officials working within. As dusk fell on the Tuesday events unfolded in the same manner, until in furious intent the inner-directed crowd gave vent to that explosive expression of themselves which brought about the wrecking of the commercial high streets of the township itself. The Tonypandy riots, as contemporaries well understood, made the industrial dispute of a different order and, in its totality, placed the name of Tonypandy alongside Peterloo, the Merthyr Rising of 1831, the Chartist March on Newport in 1839, and down to Orgreave in 1984. The State did not hold the ring in any of those encounters. It used police and soldiers to enforce the will of Property against the interests of People. One hundred years on those off-camera actions of 1910-11 in mid-Rhondda are still the stuff of pride and memory.

Of course, the faces we see in the crowd did not know then any of that which was to come to them in their lives. The Minimum Wage of 1912 which their lone struggle of 1910 presaged, the incredible solidarity of the General Strike of 1926, and the long years of unemployment sandwiched between horrific world wars, the lot of so many of the young and cocky collier boys who stare back at us through the lens. But, growing up as I did amongst the survivors of these very people in Tonypandy after 1945, it was patently clear that along with the hard experience of life endured they had become, together, conscious of playing their own part in the drama they had been handed, and determined to write their own ending. The great reforming governments that came in after 1945, had some of their origins in the impulses of 1910 and some of their greater ambitions, in the words of The Miner's Next Step, published in Tonypandy in 1912, lay in the desire to sustain a solidarity of spirit that was not "the Solidarity of sheep."

The pictures collected here by Gwyn Evans and David Maddox, to both of whom we owe a huge debt for their skill and labour, are a lasting witness to what occurred. With graphic visual literariness, they lay bare those intimate connections between coal owners and the commercial and social fabric of Tonypandy, and so underline the semaphored message the strikers were sending on that riotous night of 8 November, and on through the violent confrontations that marked the year of armed occupation which followed. Gwyn and David have been assiduous in their continuing search for written, oral and visual evidence since they worked together as two schoolteachers to create, with their pupils in Tonypandy, their prize-winning Exhibition of the 1970s. In this centenary year they have uncovered yet more material which no one has exposed before. The overall effect of the voices of the time, the stunning images then captured, and the story of place and people they tell so well and lucidly, makes this a poignant volume. But what makes it truly special is the glimpse afforded us of a past which has given many of us our undeniable cultural DNA, one which will inevitably still shape what is yet to come.

Dai Smith

The Tonypandy Riots 1910-1911

The Cambrian Combine Strike **Calendar of Events 1910-11**

1910

JUNE — Opening of new Bute Seam at Ely Pit, Penygraig.
Owners offer 1/9d for each ton of lump coal mined.
Men demand 2/6 a ton. Deadlock in negotiations.

AUGUST — Owners lock-out all miners employed at Ely Pit.

SEPTEMBER — Unofficial strike by neighbouring Naval Company collieries. Men resume work after 'Mabon' SWMF President, agrees to a coalfield conference to discuss the issues. SWMF ballot decides on an official strike at Cambrian Combine collieries from November 1st.

OCTOBER — Further negotiations by 'Mabon' with owners.
Increased offer of 2/1¾d per ton rejected by men.
Coal Owners' Association agrees to indemnify the owners of the Cambrian Combine against losses.
Miners' meeting at Empire Theatre, Tonypandy agrees a policy of mass picketing of Cambrian collieries.
Chief Constable of Glamorganshire, Captain Lionel Lindsay drafts extra police into the strike area.

NOVEMBER — 1st: Official strike begins.
7th: Miners and families successfully picket local collieries except the Glamorgan Colliery Llwynypia
Late afternoon, strikers stone the Glamorgan Colliery Powerhouse. Fierce clashes with the police.
Chief Constable requests reinforcements from the military.

NOVEMBER — 8th: Churchill, Home Secretary, stops infantry at Swindon and the cavalry at Cardiff. Sends reinforcements of Metropolitan police.
Mass meeting and march to the Glamorgan Colliery.
Further serious fighting. A miner is killed.
Stipendiary Magistrate Lleufer Thomas requests Home Office to dispatch military to the strike area. Churchill authorises the use of troops.
During the evening the town of Tonypandy ransacked and looted. Metropolitan police arrive late evening.
9th: Hussars arrive at Tonypandy to take up positions at the Glamorgan Colliery.
21st: Disturbances at Penygraig and Blaenclydach.

DECEMBER — Trial of the Gilfach miners at Pontypridd.

1910

JANUARY — Negotiations to end the strike.
SWMF concern about the financial cost of supporting the strikers.
The Combine Committee advocates drastic action to be taken against any men returning to work.

MARCH — Further violence at the Britannic Colliery Gilfach Goch.
23rd: Serious rioting at Blaenclydach. A slaughter house is gutted and a grocer's shop looted.

APRIL — Miners Federation of Great Britain raises the issue of the minimum wage and the continuance of the £3,000 weekly grant to SWMF.

MAY — 4th: Disturbances at Blaenclydach and Tonypandy.
Owners offer rejected. MFGB recommends an end to the strike and withdraws financial support.
Cambrian Strike Manifesto published.

JULY — 25th: Serious rioting at the Ely Pit, Penygraig.

AUGUST — Strike pay reduced.
Miners' leaders Will John and John Hopla summoned for alleged incitement of rioting at the Ely Pit.

SEPTEMBER — The Strike settled and men return to work.

NOVEMBER — Trial of Miners' Leaders. Will John and John Hopla jailed.

The Tonypandy Riots 1910-1911 **Who's Who**

David Alfred Thomas MP
Owner of the Cambrian Combine

Captain Lionel Lindsay
Chief Constable of Glamorganshire

Winston Churchill
Home Secretary in the Liberal Government

William Abrahams MP
'Mabon' President SWMF

William John
Miners' Leader

Leonard Llewellyn
General Manager of the Cambrian Combine

Major General Neville Macready
In charge of the military in the valleys

D. Lleufer Thomas
Stipendiary Magistrate

Keir Hardie MP
for Merthyr and Aberdare

John Hopla
Miners' Leader

The Tonypandy Riots 1910-1911 **A Coal Community**

Llwynypia and Tonypandy c1910, with the Glamorgan Collieries at the centre

A Coal Community 1900-1910

On the 9th of November, 1910 the world knew the name of Tonypandy. Newspaper headlines detailing the rioting and sacking of the Welsh Valley town defined its identity throughout the Twentieth century. But what kind of community was Tonypandy in the years before the serious breakdown of law and order and relationships? The population of the Rhondda Valley had grown rapidly in the late 1890s and particularly in the years after 1900 due to the expansion of the coal trade. The Valleys had an abundance of steam coal highly prized by the Admiralty and by merchant navies but also for needs of industry and transportation. This was the period when coal was the 'must have' fuel . Millions of tons of coal poured out from the Rhondda Valley to the ports of Cardiff and Barry for export to its world market. Coal produced such huge wealth for the coalowners and shareholders that it is often referred to as 'Black Diamonds' or 'Black Gold' .

The ever increasing demand for coal led to the sinking of many mines in the Rhondda Valleys. Several large coal companies were located in the Mid-Rhondda area; the Glamorgan, the Cambrian and the Naval. This rapidly growing industry had an insatiable need for labour and attracted young men from across Wales and parts of England in search of regular employment and high wages.

The Rhondda Valley was thus transformed from a quiet rural area in the 1850s with a population of just over a 1,000 to over 150,000 by 1911. Rhondda's population was one of the fastest growing in the world with the birth rate exceeding the figures for England and Wales. The highest birth rates were in the Tonypandy area at Clydach Vale (the Cambrian Collieries district) and at Llwynypia (the Glamorgan Colliery area).

The new migrant population pouring into the valleys urgently needed housing, which was rapidly built by speculative builders near to the collieries using local stone from hillside quarries. Terraced homes became the predominant image of the valleys. The inexact match of people to houses, inevitably resulted in over crowding where sometimes houses were shared by a family and up to six lodgers. The shift system allowed beds to be used day and night. Without pithead baths, miners had to bathe at home in a tub or zinc bath before the kitchen fire. The simple structure of the terrace lacked 'modern amenities' and flushing toilets were practically non existent.

Life for the woman managing the home and caring for a large family was particularly hard. Dirt and dust generated from the collieries nearby and the smoking chimneys of every home made the task of keeping the home clean an arduous one. But pride in keeping a 'tidy' home was reflected in what became a Valley tradition, where women scrubbed and scoured the doorsteps and the pavement in front of their houses.

Washing was done by hand using a scrubbing board, dolly and mangle. With several men in many households (husband, sons and lodgers) working in the mines, the burden of washing their clothes, heating sufficient hot water on the coal fire for baths and preparing cooked meals on their return from work, created a never-ending cycle of work for women. Overwork was responsible for the early deaths of many women.

This large and growing population needed food and goods of all kinds which led to the growth of thriving shopping centres throughout the mining valleys. At Tonypandy, there were grocers, fruiterers, fishmongers, drapers, cobblers, chemists, jewellers and even pawnbrokers for those who got into debt.

Schools flourished as a result of the influx of thousands of families and the very high birth rate. Classes were invariably large. Sunday schools continued to provide some educational instruction but by 1900, the local authority was providing a basic education for all children.

The miners and their families, as well as creating homes, worked to build many different community amenities which reflected their attitudes and values.

Over 151 chapels had been built in the Rhondda by 1905, Sunday being a very important day for many families with regular attendance at services. The chapels were amongst the visually dominant buildings in mining villages, providing a variety of leisure activities including the formation of choirs, orchestras, bands and drama groups. Local eisteddfodau and cymanfaoedd canu (hymn singing festivals) were eagerly attended with the former creating highly competitive arenas for the wealth of musical talent in the valley.

The town of Tonypandy also boasted of having three theatres offering first class entertainment with performances by the well known celebrities of the day.

Miners' Institutes acted as community centres and like the chapels were dominant buildings in the community. The Judges Hall, Tonypandy, opened in 1909, providing a concert hall, library, billiard rooms and places for meetings.

Public houses also grew rapidly and at first there was much drunkenness. This decreased in part due to the influence of the Temperance movement, the chapels and a growing interest in sport.

Tonypandy was a thriving bustling community in the years before 1910.

A Coal Community **Tonypandy: The Town**

The bustling shopping area of Tonypandy c.1910

With the rapid growth of the Rhondda's population came a great demand for shops. This was particularly so in the Mid-Rhondda area where over 12,000 men were employed in local mines earning good wages. Each village had its own shopping centre which usually stretched along both sides of the main street. Most people shopped locally but also visited Pontypridd with its important market or occasionally took the train to Cardiff.

5

A Coal Community **Tonypandy: The Town**

Pandy Square and De Winton Street in the years before 1910

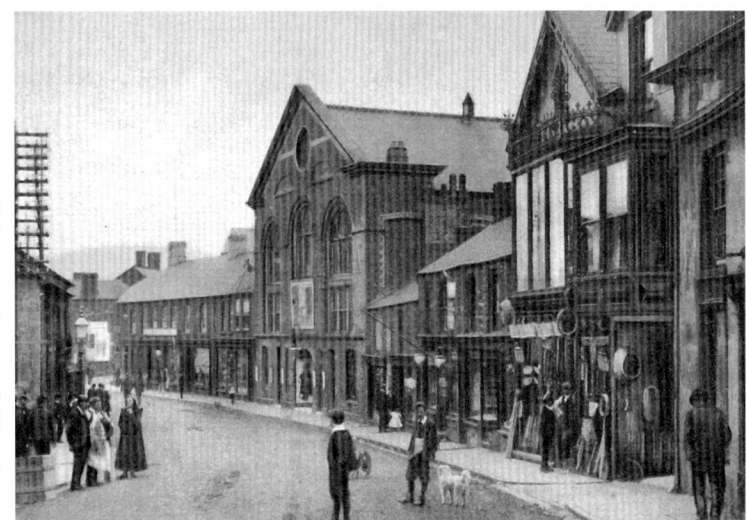

A Coal Community **Tonypandy: The Town**

EYE WITNESS: Lilly Pontsford
"You didn't see people racing to Pandy first thing in the morning. No, the work came first. Well, you see we had miners and you never knew how they are going to come home. Well, you had to keep your upstairs tidy, your beds tidy in case, you never know when a knock would come to the door, saying they were hurt or something. That was the important thing, that your upstairs to be done first. Then downstairs you'd clean and go shopping after."

Shops were an important source of local employment for young unmarried girls who would otherwise be forced to leave home to 'go into service' to work as maids or cleaners in the big houses of the rich in Cardiff and the Vale of Glamorgan.

A Coal Community Tonypandy: The Town

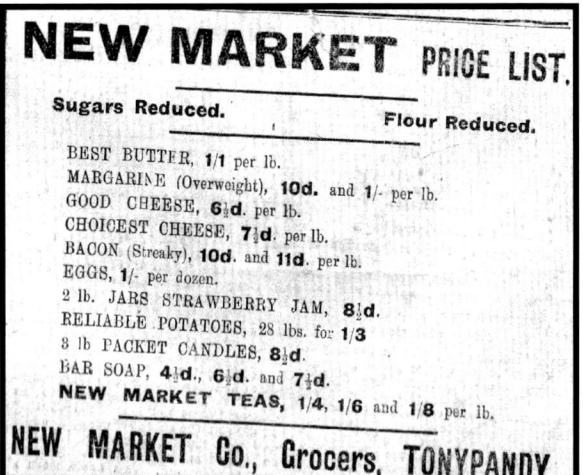

Food Prices November 1910

Shop work was hard, with long hours and low wages. Boys too young for the mines, were able to work part-time weighing goods, or delivering them to houses.

Butter, cheese and lard were delivered to shops in large pieces and had to be cut, weighed and wrapped. Tea, flour, rice, dried fruit and sugar came in sacks or boxes.

At weekends, shops would be crowded and remained open until after 11pm. Thomas and Evans at nearby Porth opened at 8am and closed at 10pm in the week and 11pm on Saturday.

'The shop smelled of wholesome things. Golden sawdust, thrown fresh every morning on the swept floor between the two long parallel counters, retained its breath of sawn trees. There was one chair for stout old women panting on arrival from up or down hilly Clydach in our wonderfully bad weather. There were lettered canisters of black on gold, an odorous coffee-grinding machine, mounds of yellow Canadian and pallid Caerphilly cheeses, rosy cuts of ham and bacon, wide slabs of butter cut by wire for the scales, and bladders of lard. Behind the counter over which my mother presided stretched wall fixtures stacked with crimson packets of tea, blue satchels of sugar, vari-coloured bags of rice, dried fruit and peas, weighed and packaged by hand out of chests and canvas sacks on quiet Mondays. Soaps gave their own clean smell, especially the flavoured kind which arrived in long bars and cut into segments which were used for both scrubbing houses and washing pit dirt from colliers' backs and fronts. Slabs of rich cake lay in a glass case on an intersecting counter stacked with biscuit tins. Packets of Ringers Tobacco, black chewing shag, spices, almonds and herbs occupied a row of drawers under the counter inside a grocer's shop.'
'Print of a Hare's Foot' by Rhys Davies

Evans the fruiterers (the author's grandparent's shop)

Dunraven Street, Tonypandy boasted a variety of shops catering for all needs

A Coal Community **Tonypandy: 'Pandy Square'**

'Pandy Square', c1908. Transport had to come to terms with newly introduced tramways

A Coal Community **Tonypandy**: Shop Advertisements

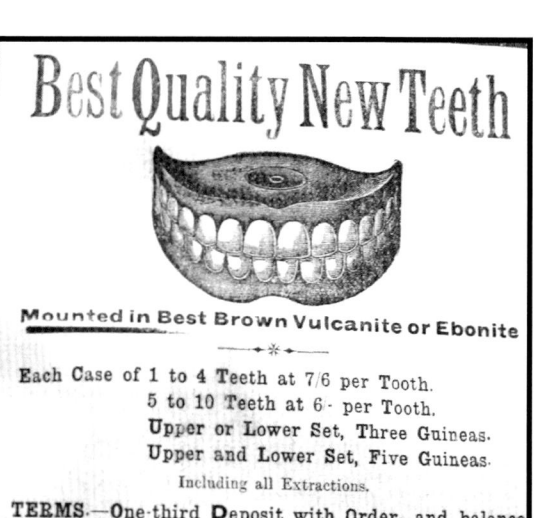

Advertisements from the local newspaper 'The Rhondda Leader', 1909-1910

A Coal Community **Tonypandy: 'Pandy Square'**

A butcher's cart being photographed outside J. Haydn Jones' Gents Hatters on 'Pandy Square' attracts a crowd and not a smile!

A Coal Community A Contrast in Living: The Coalowners

The Glyncornel House, home to Leonard Llewellyn, General Manager of the Cambrian Combine Collieries Ltd

Leonard Llewellyn

Llwyn Onn, Clydach Vale the home of the manager of the Cambrian Colliery

Maid servants who worked at the Glyncornel House

A Coal Community A Contrast in Living: The Miners

EYE WITNESS: Housewife Lilly Pontsford and her husband Arthur Pontsford a miner at the Glamorgan colliery

"You see there was no washing machines nothing of that just dollys, wooden dollys and the washing boards all by hand.

(There were) Flagstones on the floor ... no carpets on the floor ... boiling the water on the fire in a bucket ...black lead on the grate ...with big high hobs. Well you'd put the bucket on the fire.

There were five men bathing in the house. (For) a bath in front of the fire we had to warm water three times a day ... it was hard work.

Your kitchen would be stones and you'd have matting. But you wouldn't wash those stones you'd use sand. Stone and sand, you'd scour the stones. But mind you they were like milk when it was all done.

Then you'd have oilcloth in the parlour and a mat by the fire. Oh! you was the goods, you was the top. In the kitchen (there was) coconut matting on the flag stones."

Cambrian colliery miners returning home at the end of the shift

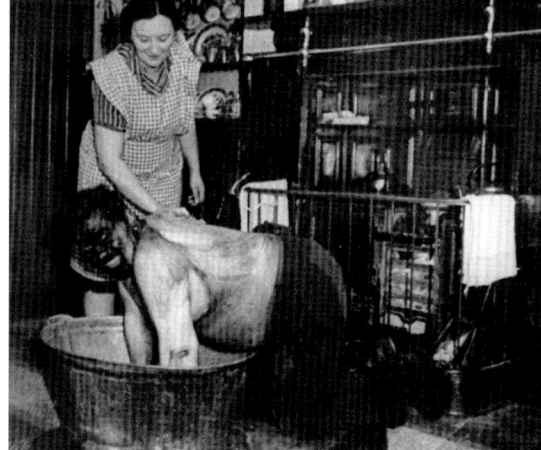

Bathing in front of the fire meant hard work for the women in boiling sufficient water and clearing up afterwards

Washing by hand using a dolly

A Coal Community **Social Life: Schools**

Problems of Attendance
These Rhondda School Log book entries from 1905 tell us about some of the problems with attendance.
March 6 'Mabon's Monday or colliers' monthly holiday seriously affects our attendance.'
May 15th 'A Gymanfa with the Methodists on Monday and a bazaar with the Baptists reduced very materially the attendance on Monday.'
July 14th 'The attendance of the week is lower than it has been for some months owing to the Sunday School outings, the accident at Wattstown and the prevalence of whooping cough and chicken pox.'

Very little real poverty *"The District is prosperous and good wages are earned. The children have generally speaking, the appearance of being well fed, and defects in clothing and boots are probably in most cases, due to carelessness or vicious habits on the part of the parents. There is very little real poverty in the district and during the year under review no case of a child suffering from this cause has been met with..."*
Medical Officer of Health Report for Rhondda 1909

The rapidly growing population of miners' families required schools to educate the children. Young miners could earn high wages earlier than in older parts of the coalfield which meant earlier marriage. The birth rate in the Mid-Rhondda area was one of the highest in Great Britain.

A Coal Community **Social Life: Chapels**

A chapel parade singing as they march through Clydach Vale in 1910. They usually displayed the chapel and temperance banners

EYE WITNESS:
"All our social life was with the chapel…there was something there every night of the week for us…

We were over 300 members. Everyone went to chapel. That was our way of life and it wasn't dull mind, we had an awful lot of fun."
Rhondda woman, born 1904

Many of the chapels were built or extended after the 'Revival' of 1904. By 1905 there were 151 chapels in the Rhondda with enough seats for nearly three quarters of the people living there.

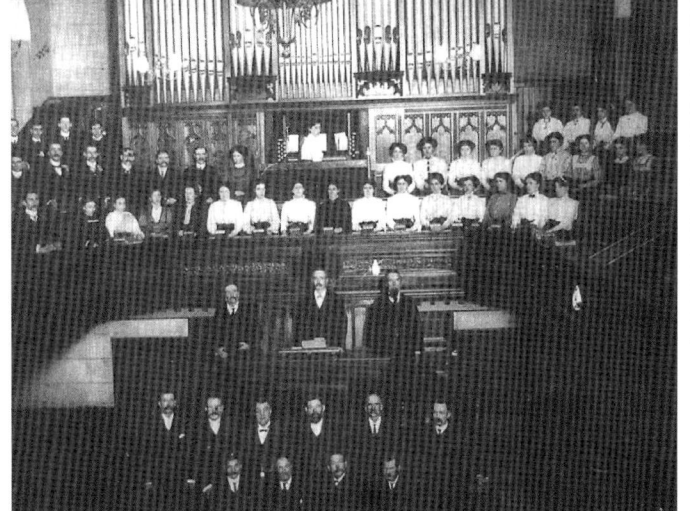
Soar Chapel, Penygraig with the minister, deacons and choir

Calfaria and Zoar Chapels, Clydach Vale

A Coal Community **Social Life: Chapels**

*The Zoar Chapel Orchestral Society, Clydach Vale in 1908.
Even small chapels had their choirs, orchestras and drama groups*

A Coal Community **Social Life: Chapels**

The Zoar Chapel Juvenile Orchestral Society, Clydach Vale in 1908

A Coal Community **Social Life: Public Houses**

The De Winton Hotel, Tonypandy. 'Pubs' were frequented by men only but provided work for young women as barmaids and maid servants

To some miners public houses were a popular 'stop' on the way home from work, particularly on pay day. (note there were no pit head baths in those days!)

The Butchers Arms, Penygraig

In 1908 in Glamorgan over 5,000 people were convicted of drunkenness and 69 publicans were prosecuted. Temperance Societies organised vigilante committees throughout the Rhondda Valley. The local newspaper regularly printed lists of 'inebriates' who had been fined sums ranging from 10/- to a £1.

A Coal Community **Social Life: Culture and Class**

Judges Hall named after Judge Gwilym Williams, whose family donated the land. It was opened by Princess Louise in 1909. It had an assembly room to seat 1,000, a workmen's institute in the basement with billiards, a lecture room and a committee room

A YMCA garden party at Tonypandy during the strike, July 1911

Penrhys Golf Club opened in 1910. Local chemist, rugby international Willie Llewellyn and his wife were prominent members

130+ strong Mid-Rhondda Choir 1905. A reflection of the great interest and commitment to musical culture in the area

A Coal Community Social Life: Theatres

The Theatre Royal

Tonypandy could boast of having 3 theatres by 1910:
The Theatre Royal, The Empire and The Hippodrome.

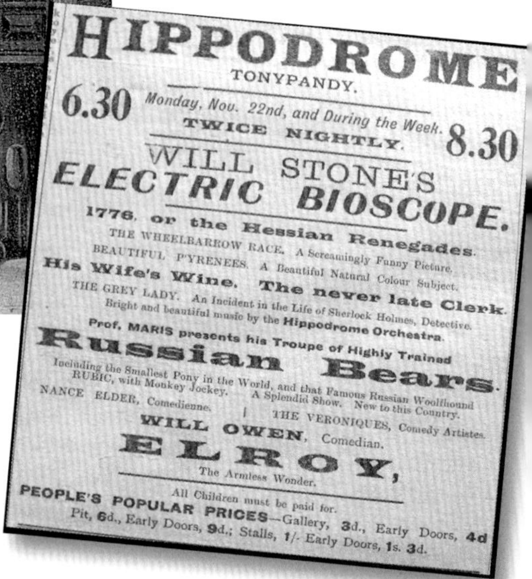

The Empire

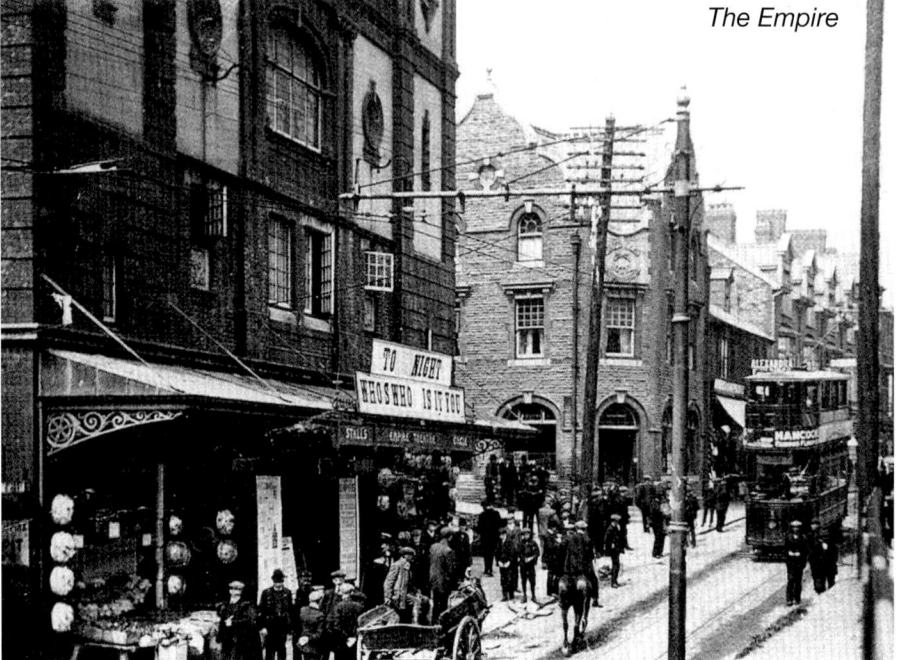

A Coal Community Social Life: Theatres

During the Cambrian Combine strike, card carrying members of the SWMF and their families were admitted at reduced prices.

THEATRE ROYAL, Tonypandy.
ELECTRIC BIOGRAPH NIGHTLY.

Monday, November 21st, and during the Week,
Mr. F. B. WOULFE & COMPANY
In a Repertoire of well-known Plays (for particulars see bills).

ALL MEMBERS OF THE MINERS' FEDERATION
(Showing their Cards),
Also their WIFES, DAUGHTERS and SWEETHEARTS
will be admitted at **3d.; 6d.; 9d. and 1/-**
Usual Prices for those not showing Cards.

The interior of the Theatre Royal Tonypandy. It also showed pictures using the new and exciting Electric Biograph

A Coal Community **Social Life: Sport**

The World Sprint Championship at Pontypridd in 1910

Sport was a strong element of community life with rugby, soccer, athletics and boxing popular pastimes for players and spectators.

Major football and rugby teams visited the Rhondda. The Australian Wallabies rugby team played Penygraig in 1908 and in the same year a northern union (rugby league) England v Wales international was held at Tonypandy in front of a 15,000 crowd. Local Tonypandy chemist, Willie Llewellyn (inset), played in the Welsh team which defeated the New Zealand All Blacks in Cardiff in 1905. He captained the triple crown winners in the same year. He also scored 4 tries in an international against England.

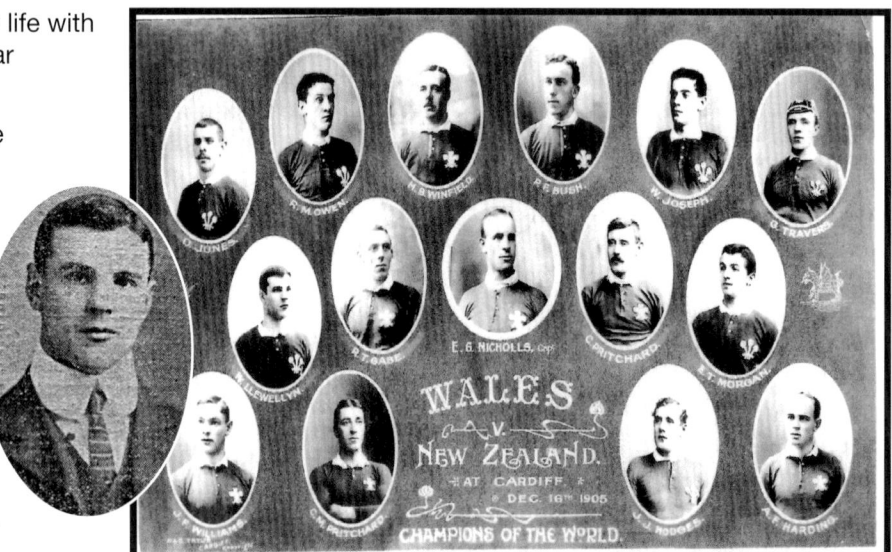

22

A Coal Community Social Life: Sport

Mid-Rhondda Athletic Grounds, Tonypandy

EASTER MONDAY & TUESDAY, April 20th & 21st, 1908.

MONDAY.—Grand Northern Union International Football Match—

ENGLAND v. WALES!

Kick Off at 3.30.

TUESDAY.—Grand Horse Racing, and Donkey Race. Trotting in Saddle and Harness, 1½ Miles. Galloway Racing, 1½ miles and 1 mile. £60 in Prizes.

GATES OPEN AT 1, FIRST RACE AT 2 O'CLOCK SHARP.

For Entry Forms, and other information, apply—

Sports Secretary, Mid-Rhondda Social & Athletic Club
TONYPANDY.

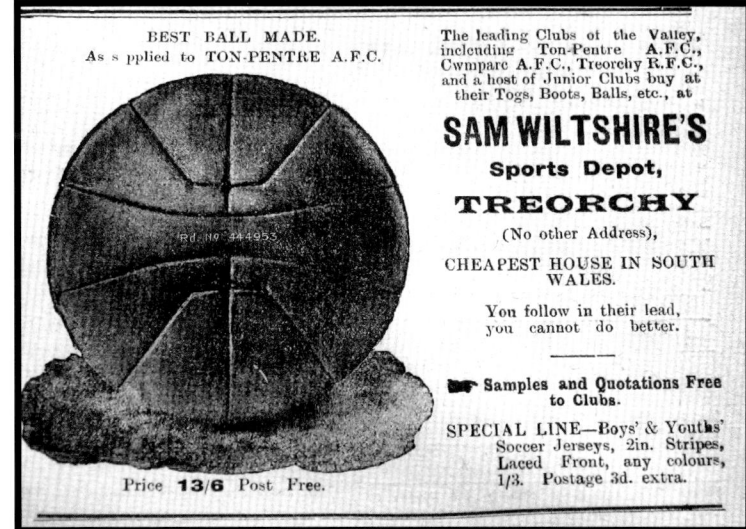

BEST BALL MADE.
As supplied to TON-PENTRE A.F.C.

The leading Clubs of the Valley, including Ton-Pentre A.F.C., Cwmparc A.F.C., Treorchy R.F.C., and a host of Junior Clubs buy their Togs, Boots, Balls, etc., at

SAM WILTSHIRE'S
Sports Depot,
TREORCHY
(No other Address),

CHEAPEST HOUSE IN SOUTH WALES.

You follow in their lead, you cannot do better.

Samples and Quotations Free to Clubs.

SPECIAL LINE—Boys' & Youths' Soccer Jerseys, 2in. Stripes, Laced Front, any colours, 1/3. Postage 3d. extra.

Price **13/6** Post Free.

Ton Pentre FC won the South Wales Cup 1907-08, 1908-09, and 1909-1910 which remains a record.

England V Wales
Great Match at Tonypandy

Prolific Scoring

Huge Crowd Delighted with Display

Thanks to the enterprise of the Mid-Rhondda Social and Athletic Club, coupled with the diplomatic foresight of the committee responsible for the arrangements of the match, Rhonddaites were treated to a game on Monday last which, judged from the spectacular point of view, has probably been unsurpassed for many years. The Northern Union code has been steadily engrossing the affections of Rhondda footballers for sometime past, and Mondays match was calculated to give the movement for establishing professional clubs in the Valleys an immense fillip. Certain it is that the enormous crowd - some 15,000 and more - were filled with delight at the character of the game.

The Rhondda Leader Report - April 1908
Wales won 35 points to 18.

A Coal Community Civic Ceremony: A Statute to Coalowner Archibald Hood July 1906

William Abrahams MP 'Mabon' addresses the crowd at the unveiling of a statue of Archibald Hood. The statue was erected outside the Llwynypia Workmen's' Library and Institute. Hood's Glamorgan collieries were taken over by David Alfred Thomas MP as part of his powerful company the Cambrian Combine Ltd

On Monday 2nd July, 1906 Federation Day (Mabon's Day) a statue to perpetuate the memory of Archibald Hood, a Scottish engineer was unveiled in the forecourt of the Llwynypia Miners' Library and Institute. Hood had been responsible for the sinking of the Glamorgan Colliery at Llwynypia in 1861. It was known locally as 'The Scotch' colliery. He built terraced housing for his workers on the hillside above the colliery.

Speakers at the ceremony claimed the event as a red letter day in the history of Mid-Rhondda. They expressed a debt of gratitude from local people to Archibald Hood for the great interest he had taken in improving the social conditions of the community and in developing the South Wales coal trade. William Abrahams MP (Mabon) led the vast crowd in singing the hymn, 'O Fryniau Caersalem' and claimed *"We know him as a friend of the working man"*.

Later on Monday 2nd July, 1906 W. W. Hood the son of Archibald Hood, attended another ceremony to officially open a swimming baths which had been erected in the terraces above the Glamorgan Colliery. The land and a free water supply had been donated by the colliery. The baths met the requirements needed to hold international races and it had laundry facilities with the latest washing machines and drying cabinets.

A Coal Community Civic Ceremony: Memorial Fountain to Coalowner Archibald Hood October 1908

October 1908. Local dignitaries assembled on the square at Tonypandy ready for the unveiling by William Abrahams MP, 'Mabon' of a water fountain and troughs with its 'Lady of the Lamp'. The 'new fountain' was paid for out of funds remaining after the erection of a monument to coalowner Archibald Hood. Other prominent members of the stage party were Leonard Llewellyn, General Manager of the Cambrian Collieries, J. Owen Jones, draper, Chairman of the local Chamber of Trade, and D. Watts Morgan, the miner's agent.

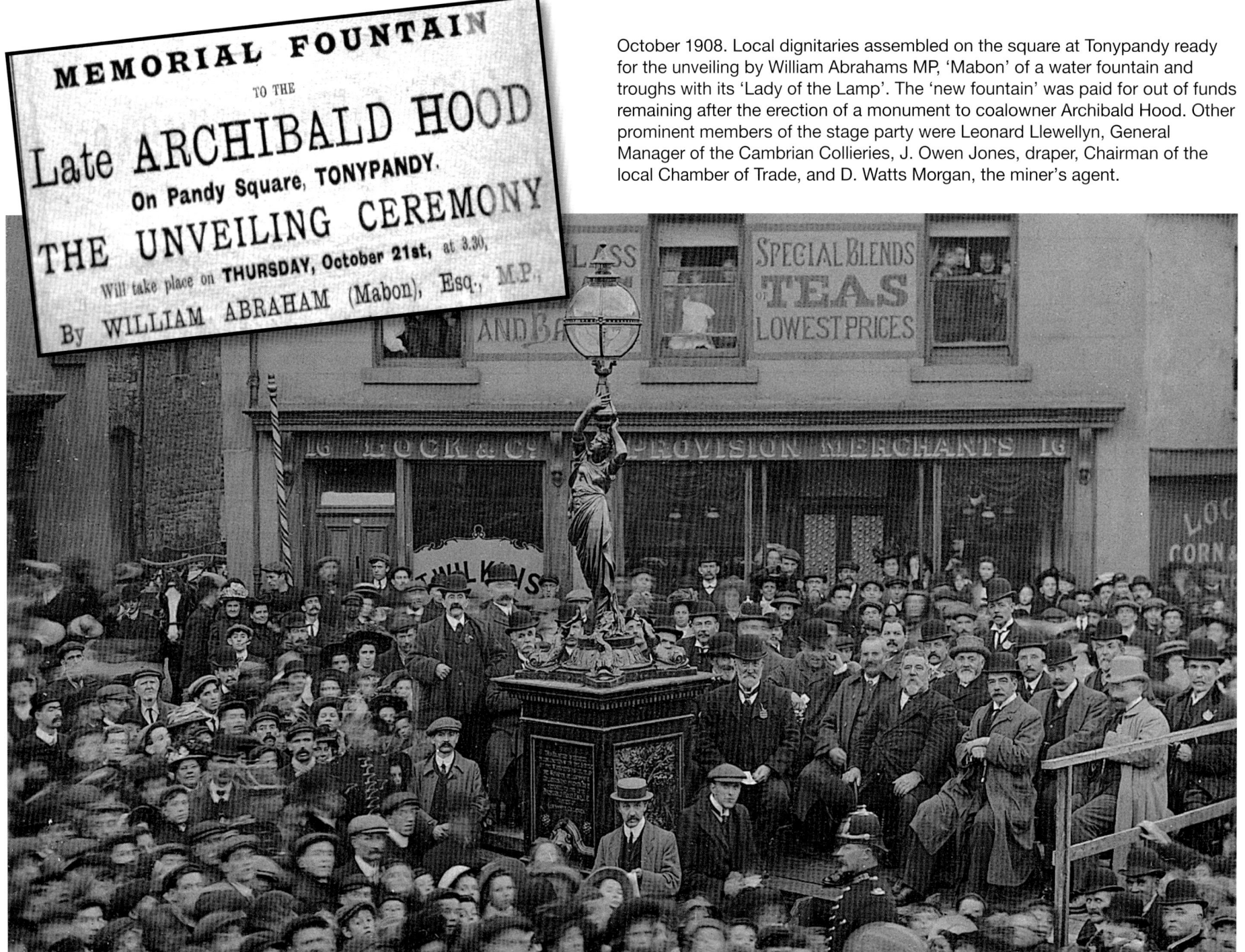

A Coal Community Tonypandy: The Other Side of Life

The rapid growth of the coal industry in the Valleys and its coal communities like Tonypandy was not without its problems. There was an acute shortage of housing for the thousands that poured into the area and the nature of the valleys led to terraced housing being built near to the coal mines with the adverse effects of a coal environment. Medical Officer of Health reports provide factual and interpretative accounts of the problems as the authorities saw them at the time.

They highlight overcrowding particularly in the cellar dwellings which were often unfit for inhabitation. The quality of water and the problem of the disposal of sewage were further concerns.

'These three months had the effect of leaving me in a state of complete amazement that any human being could be a collier. The Rhondda Valley and the river, which 50 years ago, I believe was a first class salmon river was the nearest approach to hell that I ever want to see. The river flowed jet black - it rained almost the whole time and it was often accompanied by a suffocating fog.

I could never understand why the collier went on working and why he did not seek outlet by emigration ... yet he seemed content to go down the pit, with the possibility of death. I suppose it was either tradition or environment that kept him at his job.'
'Episodes and Reflections' by Sir Wyndham Childs, a military officer sent to the Valleys during the strike.

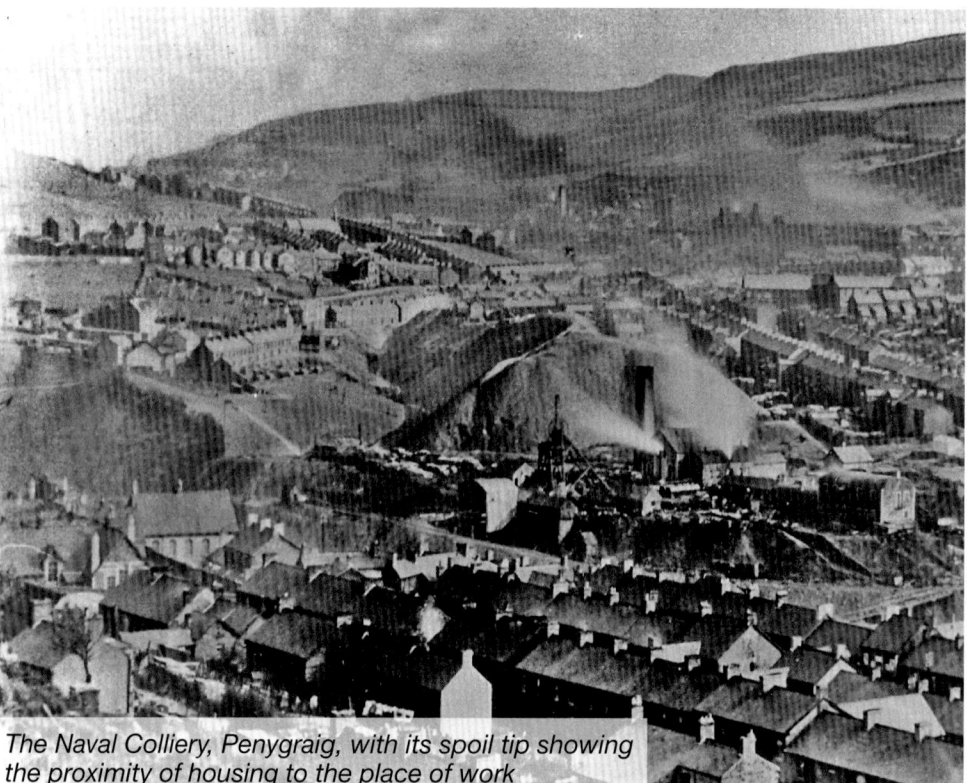
The Naval Colliery, Penygraig, with its spoil tip showing the proximity of housing to the place of work

A typical early terrace of houses in the valley

In the Shadow of the Tips
'The collieries and their tips, of the latter of which there are many in the district, and in the shadow of which a good many houses have been built, probably exercise an undesirable influence upon the habits of the people in this direction. Their dusty disordered and decidedly inartistic appearance offers no incentive to the individual householder to beautify his own home from a spirit of emulation. That much can be done towards the salubrity of his immediate surroundings by the individual possessing a 'health conscience' is sufficiently and frequently proved in the course of a day's house inspection in even the worst portions of the district. Now that the Eight Hours Act is in force and that the hours of work generally adhered to in the district permit the colliers to enjoy many hours of daylight and sunshine at home, it is hoped that their gardens and general surroundings of their houses will receive the amount of attention that is due to them, for it is certain that the time so given will be compensated for a hundredfold in the pleasure cleanliness, promotion of health, and the inculcation of good habits in self and others which such an employment of one's leisure hours would doubtless help bring in its train.'
From Report of the Medical Officer of Health 1909

A Coal Community Mining: 'The Price Paid'

The dangers of coalmining in the Rhondda were very evident to those who lived in coal communities. Every year from 1900-1910 over 50 miners died in the Valley from small mining accidents. This figure does not include major disasters such as occurred in 1905 when 119 were killed at Wattstown. The Cambrian Combine companies also suffered with 33 men killed in an explosion at Clydach Vale in 1905 and seven at one of the Naval collieries in 1907. Hundreds of miners were also injured each year and all underground workmen faced reduced life expectancy from exposure to the 'dust problem'.

Funerals of Wattstown miners in 1905. 119 miners died in an explosion

Ely Pit workmen injured in the cage accident in 1909, about to embark at Penygraig on a day's outing to Builth. The car belonged to Leonard Llewellyn, the Cambrian Combine's General Manager

Terrible Explosion at Clydach Vale

Heavy Death Roll.

Men Still Missing.

Pit a Veritable Inferno.

Scenes in the Mine.

All Hope Abandoned.

The Cambrian colliery explosion 1905

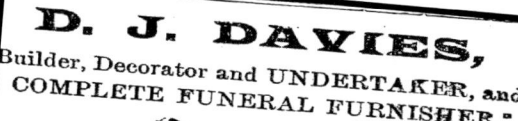

The Penygraig Disaster
Terrible Winding Accident.
Seven Killed and 21 Injured.
Graphic Narratives of Survivors.

D. J. DAVIES,
Builder, Decorator and UNDERTAKER, and COMPLETE FUNERAL FURNISHER.

Shellibiers, Hearses, Mourning and Wedding Coaches supplied on the shortest notice. Everything for Funerals supplied.

Problems of The South Wales Coalfield 1900 - 1910

The coal industry in South Wales, on which the prosperity of towns like Tonypandy depended, had expanded rapidly during the last quarter of the nineteenth century with production increasing from 16 million tons in 1870 to over 30 million tons by 1900. The years from 1900-1910, however were underlined by increasing difficulties for the Welsh steam coal industry, which faced strong competition from the USA, France and Germany. This was particularly damaging to the South Wales coal trade which had a high dependency on export markets.

Moreover a series of laws, which had been introduced to help improve the working conditions of the miners, added to costs and further reduced the profits of the coal companies. The Coal Mines Act 1896; the Workman's Compensation Act 1897, the Export Tax 1901 and new safety regulations issued by the Home Office in 1902 all impacted on the costs of production.

Even the 8 Hours Act, a piece of legislation aimed at improving miners health by shortening working hours, had the effect of reducing wages as there was less time to cut the coal. As South Wales miners had often worked considerably more hours than miners in other coalfields, (usually 10 or 10 ½ hours a shift) the impact on earnings was significant. Inflation further reduced purchasing power.

To remain competitive and to maintain profitability, coalowners looked critically at ways of reducing costs by focusing on wages, which accounted for 60% of total costs. Geological problems in the Valley's mines often made it impossible to earn a reasonable wage. This was particularly the case where the seam contained lots of stone slag, which had to be removed to get at the coal seam or where the precarious nature of the roofing required substantial safety work before attempting to win the coal or where the existence of water made mining difficult.

Miners earnings were based on the amount of lump coal they cut. The issue of their earnings in problem seams, called 'abnormal places', led to arguments with the coalowners. Miners complained that they were unable to earn a living wage when working such seams and had to go 'cap in hand' to the mine manager to try to get additions to their pay.

With the owners looking to cut costs the accepted practices of payment of allowances for work in difficult seams were drastically curtailed, inevitably affecting the relationship between colliery managers and the men.

At a regional level, there were possible conflicts from the growth of two organisations representing different interests in the coal trade. The coalowners formed the powerful South Wales and Monmouthshire Coal Owner's Association whilst the miners aimed to strengthen their position through the creation of the South Wales Miners' Federation with William Abrahams, 'Mabon', their President.

Yet the political climate was also changing in the years after 1900 and this was reflected in the election results of 1906, when 56 Labour representatives became MPs. The old Liberal consensus and conciliation approach adopted by the mens' leaders was increasingly coming under challenge. Younger lodge officials wanted a harder, less compromising approach in negotiations.

The tensions and frustrations in this coal community came to a head in 1910 when the coalowners 'locked-out' all of the men they employed at the Ely Pit, Penygraig, (part of the Cambrian Combine) over a dispute about payments for mining the newly opened Bute Seam.

A Coal Community Coal: 'The Must Have Fuel'

STILL SUPPLYING STEAM!

THE WORLD: "'Tis little Wales that keeps me spinning!"

A Western Mail cartoon of 1910 illustrates the importance of Welsh steam coal to the world economy. Rhondda supplied 1/3 of all Welsh coal, of which 50% was produced by the Cambrian Combine

Welsh coal dependence on export market

The price of South Wales coal was high due to lower productivity but the excellent quality of its steam making properties ensured a strong demand. This dependence on overseas markets made Welsh steam coal vulnerable to foreign competition.

Masters v Men

In South Wales in the 1870's, trade unionism had grown rapidly with the passage of trade union acts giving unions greater legal recognition and legalising peaceful picketing.

Strong unionism in mining was, however, slow to develop. It was not until 1898, when miners were defeated after a complete coalfield stoppage, that two local mining unions which previously had conflicting interests joined to form the South Wales Miners Federation. William Abraham (Mabon) of the Cambrian Miners' Association became President, with William Brace of the South Wales branches of the Miners' Federation of Great Britain, Vice-President. The SWMF grew rapidly to become the largest group affiliated to the MFGB with a membership of over 100,000 by 1899 (by 1914 it had over 200,000) Mabon's attitude to negotiation with the coalowners reflected his conciliatory approach and an acknowledgement of the mutual interests of owners and men.

In 1874 the coalowners, partly in response to the success of trade unionism, had formed the South Wales and Monmouthshire Coalowners Association.

Another major development during the last quarter of the nineteenth century was the amalgamation of coal companies. The most powerful of all was the Cambrian Combine founded in 1908 by David Alfred Thomas (later Lord Rhondda)

The Cambrian Coal Company Ltd., of which he was director, acquired a controlling interest in the adjoining properties of the Glamorgan Coal Company, the Naval Company Ltd., and the Britannic Merthyr Coal Company Ltd. Control was maintained by the formation of a holding company, the Cambrian Trust Company. D.A. Thomas became chairman of each of these companies. Each firm kept its identity and marketed through existing arrangements but policy was determined by the Cambrian Trust Company Board.

Historian Dai Smith comments,

"The Combine had been welded together in 1908 from existing colliery companies by D.A. Thomas, coal owner and Liberal M.P... ..It produced 50 per cent of the Rhondda's coal output and maximised profits by advanced cost-efficiency methods."

It had a vital role in both British and world trade.

In 1950 Ness Edwards MP a miners' leader wrote:

"The development of Combines was the best weapon for the enforcing of a low uniformity of prices in a particular district, and a splendid example was the activity of the Cambrian Combine..."

After the Cambrian Combine workmen gave notices to strike the Coalowner's Association agreed to support D.A. Thomas (the Combine's owner) through the imposition of a levy on all coal mined in collieries unaffected by the strike. This significantly eased the pressure on the management of the Combine in any negotiations with the men.

General Macready who was appointed as military commander in South Wales during the disturbances, commented in a letter to the Home Office on 10th December 1910, that he did not think that the strikers were feeling the effects of privation to any great extent. He was also of the opinion that the coalowners welcomed a strike that would be long enough to cause acute distress for the men as it might result in a greater period (10 years or more) free from strikes.

MASTERS v MEN

Cambrian Collieries, Clydach-Vale.

D. A. Thomas, Esq. M.P.

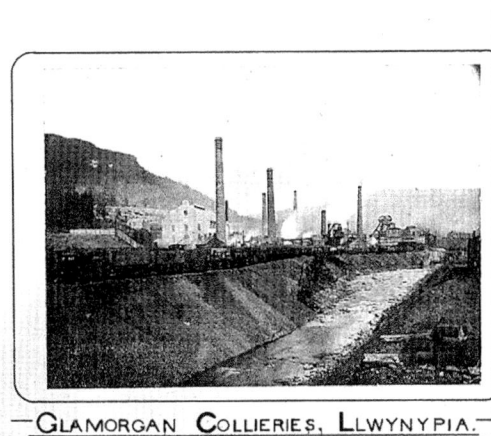

Glamorgan Collieries, Llwynypia.

Cambrian Trust

Collieries

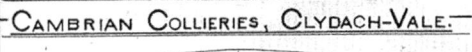

Naval Colliery, Penygraig.

L. W. Llewelyn, Esq. M.E.

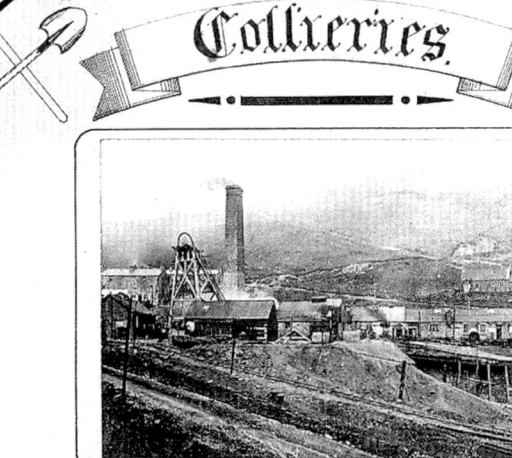

Colliery Gilfach

Harrison & Evans, Tonypandy.

— COPYRIGHT —

The Masters: Leonard Llewellyn

EYE WITNESS:
Gwen Cunningham a maid servant at Llewellyn's home gives her opinion of what it was like to work for him.

"Lovely, lovely. You wouldn't think he was the same man in the house as he was out and he never called us maids. The girls, always the girls, and the children had to obey us as well as him. If we said to do a thing, they'd have to do it. I was with him twelve years see and he used to call me 'apple face', because I had rosy cheeks. He never called me Gwen. Always 'apple cheek', always."

Leonard Llewellyn, General Manager and agent of the Cambrian Combine Collieries Ltd. was born in Aberavon and came to the Rhondda during the great strike of 1898. He rose to become a director of the Glamorgan, Naval, Britannic and Fernhill collieries.

During this time he earned a reputation for bravery. His action at the Cambrian colliery in 1900 in cutting off the steam after a boiler had exploded saved many lives. In 1905 he was awarded a silver medal by the Royal Humane Society for his heroism in the Cambrian Colliery disaster when 34 lives were lost and in the dam disaster at Clydach Vale in March 1910, he was one of the first to grapple with the situation.

To the press covering the Cambrian conflict he was 'one of the heroes of Wales'; 'a man of noble deeds and not words.'

But during the Combine strike he represented the 'Masters', who were blamed for the dispute caused by their action in locking-out all the workmen employed at the Ely colliery, Penygraig.

In the early days of the strike, Llewellyn requested police reinforcements to protect the collieries and his home. The Glamorgan Colliery with its important Powerhouse became ' a fortress' with over 100 policemen guarding it.

On the evening of 8th November, when the looting of Tonypandy occurred no policemen were on duty in the town, as they were protecting the coalowners' properties.

During the strike Leonard Llewellyn cleverly cultivated the press through his personal secretary (a former press man) as a propaganda weapon to discredit the miners, particularly over the treatment of the horses still left underground in the early weeks of the strike.

Historian Dai Smith describes him as one of the most ruthless coal operators of the time.

Masters v Men **The Coalowners**

The powerful coalowners. The South Wales and Monmouthshire Coalowner's Association was formed in 1874 (D.A. Thomas owner of the Cambrian Combine Ltd. front row third from right). The Association took strong action in support of D.A. Thomas by agreeing to indemnify his companies from losses incurred during the strike by placing a levy on all coal mined in Association mines

Masters v Men The Cambrian Combine Collieries Ltd

THE CAMBRIAN COMBINE EMPLOYEES, 1910

(i)	**Naval Colliery** Ely, Nantgwyn, Anthony, Pandy, and Adare pits	2,144
(ii)	**Cambrian Collieries**	4,054
(iii)	**Glamorgan Coal**	3,950
(iv)	**Britannic Merthyr Coal**	697
	Total	10,845

The Glamorgan Collieries, Llwynypia, known locally as 'The Scotch'

Cambrian Collieries, Clydach Vale

Cardiff Bay today, a sign from the past

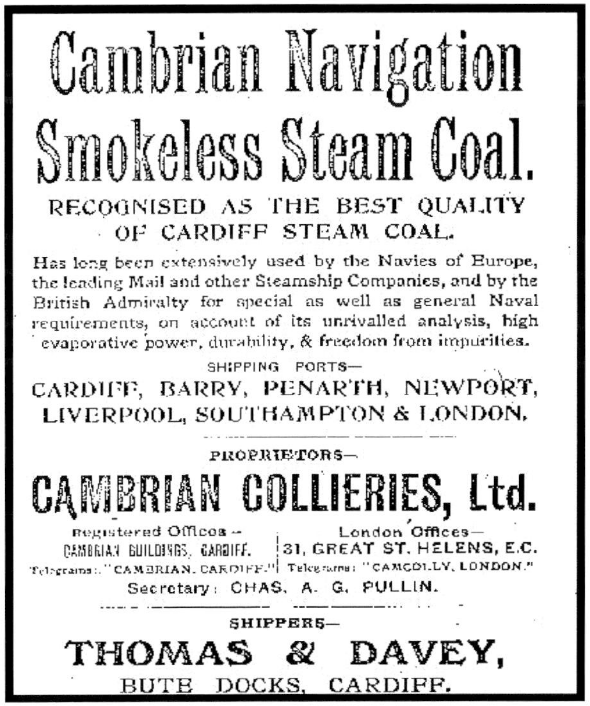

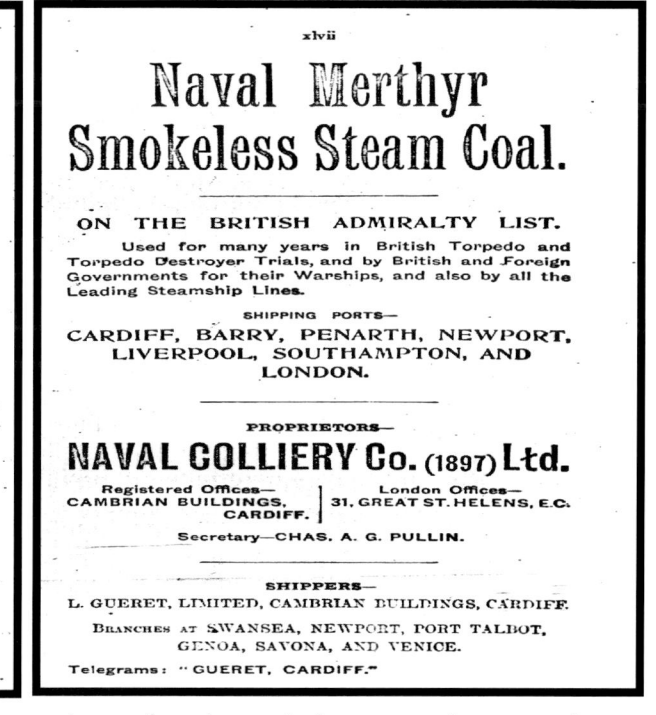

Cambrian Navigation Smokeless Steam Coal.

RECOGNISED AS THE BEST QUALITY OF CARDIFF STEAM COAL.

Has long been extensively used by the Navies of Europe, the leading Mail and other Steamship Companies, and by the British Admiralty for special as well as general Naval requirements, on account of its unrivalled analysis, high evaporative power, durability, & freedom from impurities.

SHIPPING PORTS—
CARDIFF, BARRY, PENARTH, NEWPORT, LIVERPOOL, SOUTHAMPTON & LONDON.

PROPRIETORS—
CAMBRIAN COLLIERIES, Ltd.

Registered Offices— | London Offices—
CAMBRIAN BUILDINGS, CARDIFF. | 31, GREAT ST. HELENS, E.C.
Telegrams: "CAMBRIAN, CARDIFF." | Telegrams: "CAMCOLLY, LONDON."
Secretary: CHAS. A. G. PULLIN.

SHIPPERS—
THOMAS & DAVEY,
BUTE DOCKS, CARDIFF.

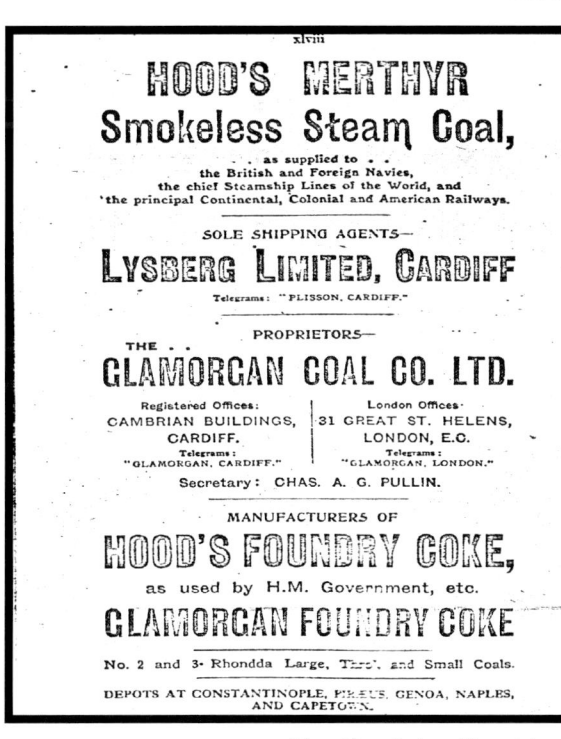

HOOD'S MERTHYR Smokeless Steam Coal,

.. as supplied to ..
the British and Foreign Navies,
the chief Steamship Lines of the World, and
the principal Continental, Colonial and American Railways.

SOLE SHIPPING AGENTS—
LYSBERG LIMITED, CARDIFF
Telegrams: "PLISSON, CARDIFF."

PROPRIETORS—
THE ..
GLAMORGAN COAL CO. LTD.

Registered Offices: | London Offices:
CAMBRIAN BUILDINGS, CARDIFF. | 31 GREAT ST. HELENS, LONDON, E.C.
Telegrams: "GLAMORGAN, CARDIFF." | Telegrams: "GLAMORGAN, LONDON."
Secretary: CHAS. A. G. PULLIN.

MANUFACTURERS OF
HOOD'S FOUNDRY COKE,
as used by H.M. Government, etc.
GLAMORGAN FOUNDRY COKE

No. 2 and 3· Rhondda Large, Thro', and Small Coals.

DEPOTS AT CONSTANTINOPLE, PIRAEUS, GENOA, NAPLES, AND CAPETOWN.

Naval Merthyr Smokeless Steam Coal.

ON THE BRITISH ADMIRALTY LIST.

Used for many years in British Torpedo and Torpedo Destroyer Trials, and by British and Foreign Governments for their Warships, and also by all the Leading Steamship Lines.

SHIPPING PORTS—
CARDIFF, BARRY, PENARTH, NEWPORT, LIVERPOOL, SOUTHAMPTON, AND LONDON.

PROPRIETORS—
NAVAL COLLIERY Co. (1897) Ltd.

Registered Offices— | London Offices—
CAMBRIAN BUILDINGS, CARDIFF. | 31, GREAT ST. HELENS, E.C.
Secretary—CHAS. A. G. PULLIN.

SHIPPERS—
L. GUERET, LIMITED, CAMBRIAN BUILDINGS, CARDIFF.

Branches at SWANSEA, NEWPORT, PORT TALBOT, GENOA, SAVONA, AND VENICE.

Telegrams: "GUERET, CARDIFF."

The Cambrian Combine was made up of, and operated as, separate companies but used the same administrative and marketing offices at the docks in Cardiff.

Ely Pit 'Lock-Out' August 1910

It was a dispute at the Ely Pit, Penygraig in August 1910 (part of the Naval group of Collieries) which was to spark the major confrontation with D.A. Thomas MP, owner of the Cambrian Combine Company Ltd. A problem arose over rates of pay in mining a newly opened seam, the Bute Seam which the men claimed was a difficult one to mine because it had many abnormal places.

'Abnormal places' were common to mines in South Wales and coalfields in England but a problem which had become more acute in the decade before the First World War. An abnormal work place was one where a diligent collier was unable to cut enough lump coal to earn a living wage. This was due to conditions beyond his control, such as geological faulting, roofing problems, the amount of slag stone which had to be removed to get at the coal or the amount of water he had to work in.

The Ely Pit management, after a trial period, offered the men working on the Bute seam 1/9 a ton of coal mined, whereas the men's representatives pressed for 2/6 a ton. At the beginning of August 1910 after lengthy negotiations without agreement, the owners posted 'lock-out' notices. They were issued not only to the 70 miners involved with the trial seam but to the entire workforce of seven hundred miners. D.A.Thomas the owner of the Cambrian Combine informed the press that,

> 'As is almost invariably the case when a new seam is opened in South Wales the men were working the Ca'Canny' in order to prove the seam was a difficult one to work...'

If during the trial workings the miners could only produce a small output of coal per ton, this would influence the referees appointed to fix and arrange a list, and would gain for them a better cutting price.

He further justified his company's action in closing down the pit by pointing out that two of the major seams being worked at the Ely Pit were approaching exhaustion. This meant that in order to maintain satisfactory profits the new seam would have to be brought into full operation at the rates offered by the company.

Tom Smith one of the miners' leaders addressing the Ely workmen provided a very different viewpoint:

> "A man working at top speed could never turn out more than six drams a day, in certain places it was only possible (to fill) 4 drams. The new price list gave no guarantee of a living wage. Wages were less than before the 8 hours bill.'"

The miners' leaders were also aware that the price accepted at the Ely Pit would influence the price paid on the Bute seam in other collieries as the seam ran throughout the valley. They knew that it was in the owners' interests to keep the price per ton as low as possible, for if there was a similar dispute in other pits, it could be pointed out that the price had already been accepted by the men at Ely, Penygraig.

The 'lock-out' led to sympathy strikes in September by the miners employed in neighbouring pits belonging to the Naval Colliery Company. William Abrahams 'Mabon', the miners' union leader appealed to them to return to work as they had not served notice of their action. A resumption of work was agreed on condition that 'Mabon' called a SWMF conference.

Members of the SWMF were balloted and as a result a decision was taken to call out on strike from November 1st 1910 all miners employed in the Cambrian Combine Collieries Ltd. (some 12,0000 men). They were to be supported with strike pay from Federation funds.

A resolution was passed which condemned

> '…the tyrannical action of the Cambrian Combine in locking out our fellow-workmen, and endeavouring through their sufferings to force upon them the acceptance of an unfair price- list.' It went on to call for 'resistance at all costs.'

PRICE LIST DISPUTE AT PENYGRAIG
Over a Thousand Men Idle
The whole of the workmen, 1000 in number employed at the Ely Pit of the Naval Collieries, Penygraig ceased work on Wednesday on the termination of the notices tendered to them on the 1st Aug. Efforts have been made to avert a stop- page but so far without success. Neither the management or the workmen will recede from the positions they have taken up. The chief cause of the dispute is failure to settle a price list in what is known as the Bute Seam. The dispute commenced about 18 months ago. The men are holding out for 2/6 per ton   The Rhondda Leader, August 1910

THE ELY PIT LOCK-OUT
August 1910

Ely Pit 'Lock-Out' August 1910 The Leader: William Abrahams 'Mabon'

William Abraham, better known to his contemporaries by his bardic name 'Mabon', was a major figure in Rhondda and South Wales mining unionism for over 40 years. Originally from Port Talbot, he moved to the Rhondda in 1875 to become a Miners' Agent taking decisions and negotiating on the men's behalf. In that year he negotiated the introduction of the Sliding Scale of Payment for miners, which related wages to the selling price of coal and was aimed at benefiting the miners.

In 1898 he became the first President of the newly formed South Wales Miners Federation.

Mabon was elected as a Liberal Member of Parliament for one of the Rhondda seats becoming the first miners' representative from South Wales.

His approach to industrial disputes favoured conciliation and industrial peace, with the strike weapon to be used only as a last resort. The events in the troubled coalfields of South Wales before the First World War saw his philosophy on industrial relations severely challenged by a new generation of younger men in the lodges of the SWMF. They did not share Mabon's conciliatory approach which was looked upon as a 'sell-out' to the coal owners. They viewed the coalowners as pursuing policies of exploitation with wages kept deliberately low to ensure higher profits. The events of Tonypandy in 1910 highlighted the differences which existed between Mabon's approach and the attitudes of the younger lodge officials.

This gulf between the leadership and the miners can clearly be seen from the following exchanges at a meeting of the Naval Company workmen discussing the unofficial stoppage in support of the Ely miners. Mabon addressing the meeting tried to persuade the men to return to work as they had not given the required month's notice of their intention to strike. He said,

> "My friend D.A. Thomas has been suffering from poor health: and I feel sure that on his holiday in France he will not benefit in health if he were to hear of such a strike as this. I beg you to hold your hand."

For the men Will Mainwaring a member of the Cambrian Lodge quickly responded:

> "Mr. D.A. Thomas may be your friend, Mr. Abrahams; he is not our friend. But we have heard your plea. We will call off the strike, but on one condition."

The condition was that as President of the SWMF Mabon should call a coalfield conference to discuss the mid-Rhondda problems. This was agreed and meant that the issue would no longer be local in character.

Later in the month of October 1910, after the miners had balloted and tendered notices to strike from November 1st, Mabon succeeded in obtaining an improved offer on the cutting price from 1/9d. per ton to 2/1¾d. per ton, but these terms were rejected by the men.

During the strike Mabon's role was overshadowed by the younger leaders such as Will John and John Hopla, members of the Cambrian Workmen's Committee. The fact that Mabon had little sympathy with socialism, the strike weapon and militant unionism, meant a widening gulf between national and local leaders.

In May 1911 Mabon made a further appeal to the men to accept the terms previously negotiated, but his eloquence was no longer able to sway this new generation of workmen who had sacrificed so much during the previous seven months.

The Cambrian Combine Strike was a watershed in his career, for it signified the end of his leadership in unionism in South Wales. In September 1911 he was overwhelmingly defeated by C.B. Stanton for a seat on the Executive Committee of the International Miners' Federation. In March 1912, six months after the ending of the Cambrian Strike, he resigned the Presidency of the South Wales Miners' Federation.

He remained a Member of Parliament until 1920. He died in 1922.

Ely Pit 'Lock-Out' August 1910 'The Lock-Out': The Issues

"The Company has to make satisfactory profits and to do this the new seam would have to be brought into full operation at the rates offered ... the company's offer is 1/9p a ton."
D.A.Thomas, the Coalowner

David Alfred Thomas was the son of a coalowner and through his family's interests in the Cambrian collieries he set about restructuring the coal industry. Through a series of take-overs he created the powerful Cambrian Colliery Company Ltd in 1908 employing over 12,000 men. His company produced over half the output of Rhondda's steam coal. He was very successful, becoming one of the wealthiest industrialist in the world.

Earlier in the decade he won the support of the miners when he criticized the Coalowner's Association but the Ely pit 'lock-out' and the all-out strike against his Cambrian Coal Company saw him become their arch enemy.

He was a Liberal MP for Merthyr Tydfil, 1888-1910 a seat where he topped the poll even when Keir Hardie was standing. In 1910 he won a seat in Cardiff. He was created Viscount Rhondda in 1915 for his work during the war.

"This is a very difficult seam to mine. A man working at top speed could never turn out more than six drams a day, in certain places it was only possible (to fill) 4 drams. The new price list gave no guarantee of a living wage'... We need to be paid 2/6d a ton." Tom Smith local miners' leader

Ely Pit 'Lock-Out' August 1910 **Miners' Views About 'Abnormal Places'**

EYE WITNESSES

"If the price list had been accepted then it would have been the price throughout the valley for this seam. The owners wanted to keep the price as low as possible, for if there was a similar dispute in other pits the owners could point out that the price had been accepted by the men of Ely, Penygraig"

"If you didn't earn enough for a living wage you had to go cap in hand to the manager to put your case. Sometimes you had something, but often you got nothing."

Ben Davies, a hitcher at the Cambrian Colliery summed up the dispute in this way.

"Sometimes you couldn't fill a dram in abnormal places. They used screen drams which were practically open at the ends, and there were bars on the sides. You couldn't keep small in it, this was waste …you were only paid for lump."

Harry Hobbs, a miner at the Cambrian Colliery.

"I've known men working on a difficult seam who didn't earn enough to pay their butty…you had to pay the boy no matter what, then, it was up to you to fight for yours afterwards."

Charles Towells, a miner at the Glamorgan Colliery, describes the predicament of working in an 'abnormal place'.

Ely Pit 'Lock-Out' August 1910 **The Sympathy Strike**

Workmen from the Naval collieries at Penygraig strike in sympathy with the 800 men 'locked-out' at the Ely Pit

SOUTH WALES MINERS' FEDERATION.

NO. 1 RHONDDA DISTRICT MEETING.

"MABON'S" APPEAL.

ADVISES THE MEN TO RETURN TO WORK.

Ely Pit 'Lock-Out' August 1910 **Mabon Continues Negotiations**

William Abrahams, 'Mabon', President of the South Wales Miners' Federation outside the Board of Trade in London. He succeeded in obtaining an improved offer for each ton of coal mined from the newly opened Bute seam but the terms were rejected by the workmen

Ely Pit 'Lock-Out' August 1910 **The Strike is Called**

Young miners at the Glamorgan Colliery, Llwynypia, taking home their tools in preparation for the start of the official strike of all the Cambrian Combine collieries, to commence on 1st November, 1910

Policing The Leaders: Captain Lionel Lindsay

Captain Lionel Lindsay succeeded his father as the Chief Constable of Glamorgan. He had previously been a major with the Egyptian gendarmerie.

It was his responsibility to make plans for any eventualities which might result from strike action in both the Rhondda and Aberdare valleys.

An incident at Aberdare on 2nd November, when a train carrying colliers was attacked by strikers and a request from the coal-owners for additional protection led the Chief Constable to draft into the strike areas every available man in the county. He also arranged for re-enforcements from neighbouring forces from Bristol.

The Chief Constable anticipated trouble in the Valleys and accordingly telegraphed the Home Office of the situation, which they received on Tuesday November 8th.

Even with reinforcements, Lindsay did not have enough men to garrison all of the collieries of the Cambrian Combine. After consultation with Leonard Llewellyn, the Combine's General Manager he placed the bulk of his forces at the Glamorgan Colliery Llwynypia, to defend the vitally important Powerhouse.

After the serious disturbances outside, 'the Glamorgan' on the evening of Monday 7th November when his force of over a hundred men, including mounted police, struggled in the confrontation with the miners, he telegraphed the army for support. Churchill's intervention led to the military being temporarily held back but after the looting of Tonypandy and a further urgent request from Lindsay and the local magistrates for the military, the Home Secretary gave the necessary authorisation.

Socially Lindsay had a close relationship with Leonard Llewellyn the Combine's General Manager but was highly critical of the young leaders of the Workmen's Joint Committee whom he described as dangerous men.

At his retirement after 46 years as Chief Constable he was presented with an illuminated address by his officers which stated,

> *"Your principal aims in the steps you took to preserve law and order were always approved and commended by the peaceful residents of the County. We who were with you (at Tonypandy 1910-11) know that but for your consistent action considerable damage to property would have resulted and the ratepayers of Glamorgan would have been penalised."*

Captain Lionel Lindsay, Chief Constable of Glamorganshire

Policing **Reinforcements Arrive In The Strike Area**

November 1st 1910. The first day of the strike. Police arrive in Tonypandy carrying their bedding

Policing **Guarding the Glamorgan Colliery**

> "All the available police in this County are now concentrated in the Aberdare Valley and Rhondda Valley, and everyone is awaiting the issue of tomorrow's important conferences."
>
> Telegram to Home Office from (Lionel Lindsay - Chief Constable of Glamorgan - November 6th 1910)

'Fortress Glamorgan' A heavy police presence at the gateway to the Glamorgan Colliery. The Chief Constable, Lionel Lindsay set-up his headquarters at the colliery, together with over 100 policemen including mounted police. If there was to be a confrontation, it was more likely to take place at the Glamorgan Colliery than in any other part of the Combine.

Policing **Guarding the Powerhouse**

Tea break for police guarding the machinery inside the Powerhouse. Leonard Llewellyn watches from the staircase.

The Powerhouse became the target for stone throwers showering officials with glass and making working conditions impossible.

It was an appeal from the general manager about the impossibility of his officials operating the powerhouse because of stone throwing, which led the Chief Constable to order the first baton charge on Monday 7th November, 1910.

The Glamorgan Colliery Powerhouse Built in 1905, it was of critical importance in the dispute. Within a complex of buildings the owners had installed a huge pumping plant which dealt with between 4,000-5,000 gallons of water per minute. The plant was electrically operated, power being supplied from a large generator erected in the colliery yard. If for any reason the plant was forced to stop, it would have meant that the number two pit would have become flooded, and would probably never re-open.

It also provided electricity for neighbouring collieries.

Policing Contingents Sent to the Valleys

POLICE CONTINGENTS SENT INTO THE RHONDDA and CYNON VALLEYS 1910 – 1911

Metropolitan 902
Glamorganshire 216
Carmarthenshire 45
Monmouthshire..................41
Gloucestershire..................26
Breconshire........................11
Cardiff City.......................101
Bristol City 63
Swansea 43
Merthyr Tydfil 31
Newport 20

Total 1, 499

The greatest number engaged at any one time was 1,301 on the 15th and 16th November, 1910.

The attitude of local people to the police can be gauged by the comment made by Moylan, Churchill's personal representative in the Valleys in his report of 23rd November, 1910, It concerned a request for the return of the Bristol detachment for the impending general Election duties,

"Bristol police can well be spared because of their exceptional unpopularity here."

Policing 'The Locals on Duty!'

Captain Lionel Lindsay drafted every available policeman under his command into the strike areas by the first week of November, some two hundred and sixteen men

Policing **Protecting Colliery Property**

Police protection for Leonard Llewellyn and his officials who worked as stokers to keep the Powerhouse working

Two officials who continued to work are given protection by a police escort

Mounted police patrol outside the Glamorgan Colliery, Llwynypia

Over 100 policemen guard the large complex of the Glamorgan Colliery

Policing Confrontation: Attacks on Colliery Officials Homes

Crowds gather outside an officials home

Homes of managers, under managers and other colliery officials were attacked. Families of these officials including Leonard Llewellyn's children were moved out of the area. During the early part of the strike the eight daughters of Evan Williams the under manager of the Naval colliery were dispersed to other members of the family for their safety.

At the William's family home plush furniture and mirrors were turned to the wall as strikers poked long poles with hooks on the end through the downstairs windows to try to rip the furniture.

Unseen by the strikers a journalist living nearby moved his valuables through the attic to the house next door for safe keeping in case his house was attacked.

Report by General Macready to Winston Churchill
'19th November 1910 the newspaper accounts are extremely exaggerated and except in a few isolated cases the damage to houses has been confined to broken panes of glass and the injuries to the people to bruises. I suggested to the Chief Constable a few days ago that in my opinion house breaking and molestation of persons at a distance be ignored.'

EYE WITNESS: Sarah Ann Jones
Attacks on the homes of colliery officials
"At no. 39 Pontrhondda, lived a colliery official, William Howells. He used to go to work at the Glamorgan Colliery by going out through his back door, down the bank by the river into the colliery. The men came down to his house to take revenge. My brother went out on the doorstep and he heard the men saying 'We don't need ammunition, there's plenty here.' At the time they were making up the road, they had been putting stones to bury because it was a field here. It was very frightening to see and hear the crowd outside. We didn't go out because you didn't know what they were going to do. They smashed all the windows and knocked the door in. Mrs Williams had left the house with her children that morning to go to Swansea. She stayed away for about 12 months and when she came back after things had settled, she saw the house as the rioters had left it, she partly cleaned but she couldn't face it - she broke her heart. They went to live in Campbell Terrace - she didn't live long afterwards.

The incident took place in the evening, next morning they painted 'blackleg' on the house. One day the police were outside in the cold and my mother said 'I'll give them a cup of tea,' but my brother said 'Mam perhaps our house...'"

The children of Leonard Llewellyn, General Manager of the Cambrian Combine in the charge of a governess and butler and under police escort leaving Llwynypia station

Mass Picketing: The First Week of The Strike (November 1910)

During the first week of November miners of the Cambrian Combine held mass meetings to discuss the tactics to be used in conducting the strike, given that the Cambrian Combine Company had been promised financial support from fellow members of the Coal Owners' Association of South Wales and Monmouthshire. Levies were to be placed on coal produced in the unaffected mines in South Wales and given to the Rhondda coalowners who as a result could hold out indefinitely. The strikers' position was considerably weaker as they and their families would have to exist on small sums of strike pay provided by the South Wales Miners Federation supported by the Miners Federation of Great Britain.

At a packed meeting of strikers at the 2000 seater Empire theatre, Tonypandy, a significant decision was taken to commit the strikers to use the tactic of mass picketing at all of the Combine's collieries with the intention of preventing all men including officials from working.

If the policy was effective it would succeed in stopping the working of the ventilation systems and the water pumps at the collieries and resulted in flooding and destruction of underground workings. The weakness of this action was the possible loss of livelihoods where seams could not be re-opened when the strike ended. The miners leaders felt that they had little option in the circumstances and this was the only means they had to put pressure on the owners and to prevent any work continuing underground.

Of critical importance in this confrontation would be the Glamorgan Colliery at Llwynypia, which employed over 3,000 men. Its Powerhouse controlled a huge pumping plant which extracted between 4,000-5,000 gallons of water per minute from the underground working. It would be a prime target. Stopping the electrically operated plant would result in immediate flooding of the underground workings and the mining of coal would become impossible.

The Chief Constable, Lionel Lindsay, after discussions with Leonard Llewellyn made the Glamorgan colliery his headquarters with a very strong police presence of over 100 officers, including mounted police.

Cambrian Combine miners leaving a meeting held at the Empire theatre Tonypandy during the first week of November. The meeting decided that mass picketing would take place at all of the Combine's collieries

"It is our intention to stop any man from doing any work at the collieries. We intend to prevent any of the officials from Mr. Llewellyn downwards from entering the colliery yard."

MASS PICKETING

Mass Picketing The Leaders: Will John and John Hopla

William John, Chairman of the Workmen's Joint Committee

William John was a powerful figure during the dispute as Chairman of the Combine's Workmen's Committee. He was a local councillor and chapel deacon.

He was jailed for a year after the Ely Pit riot of July 1911. Although the sentence was later commuted to six months.

In 1920 he was elected as a Member of Parliament for Rhondda.

Cambrian Combine Collieries Joint Committee

William John and John Hopla were young leaders of the strike which they controlled through the Cambrian Workmen's Joint Committee. Their aim was to widen the dispute and to have the central issue of abnormal places discussed throughout the coalfields. Their approach to managing the dispute conflicted with the views of Mabon and the 'old leadership'. Even as late as March 1911 when considerable pressure was being placed on them by the MFGB to settle the dispute they continued to try to widen the conflict. The bitterness towards the MFGB was shown in the way their representatives were treated on a visit to Tonypandy in March 1911.

Rail crash at Pontypridd March 1911 killing 3 members of the SWMF Executive. John Hopla was elected to one of the vacant seats

John Hopla

John Hopla, a checkweigher at the Glamorgan Colliery, was one of the best known leaders of the Rhondda miners. He was Chairman of the Glamorgan Lodge and came to prominence during the Cambrian Combine strike.

He was considered by the police to be a very dangerous man because of his influence over the workmen. He was summoned on two occasions during the strike. On the first occasion he was fined and cautioned. He was later jailed for a year with William John after the Ely Pit Riot of July 1911.

He became a member of the Executive of the SWMF in 1911, after a tragic rail accident at Pontypridd resulted in the death of 14 people, including three Rhondda members of the SWMF Executive.

After serving six months imprisonment he and William John were released and each received a heroes' welcome back in the Mid-Rhondda. Hopla died a year after his release. A plaque was unveiled to him on the local Institute Library building at Llwynypia.

Mass Picketing Officials and Blacklegs Stoke the Boilers

Leonard Llewellyn, the Combine's General Manager and his colliery officials took over stoking duties during the first few weeks of the strike, Their aim was to try to keep the boilers and engine houses working to ensure that the ventilation system and the water pumps underground continued to operate.

Leonard Llewellyn and one of his officials take a break from stoking duties

Mass Picketing **Officials Working at The Glamorgan Colliery**

The picketing of the Combine's collieries was very successful and work stopped in all except the Glamorgan Colliery, Llwynypia. The latter was well guarded by a large contingent of policemen and came to be referred to as 'Fortress Glamorgan'. Leonard Llewellyn and his officials, helped by stokers coming off ships at Cardiff, kept the ventilation and pumping machinery working.

Mass Picketing The Use of 'Black-Leg' Labour

Offers of Help to Mr. Llewelyn.

Mr. Leonard Llewelyn, who has held the fort at the Glamorgan Colliery powerhouse ever since Sunday night, received the following telegram on Wednesday:—

Provided escort to the colliery, ten, twenty or more members of the Cardiff Exchange ready to come to help you any work you suggest. Telegraph reply to ——, Mount Stuart Square, Cardiff.

The telegram was signed by a well-known Cardiff shipowner.

Mr. Llewelyn immediately telephoned the following reply:—

My co-officials and myself deeply appreciate your sympathetic telegram indicating as it does that public opinion is on our side, and we shall certainly avail ourselves of your splendid efforts if necessity arises.

LEONARD LLEWELYN.

liery Offices.

Mr. Llewelyn, in reply to our representative, stated that his company had stokers in readiness in Cardiff and other places to come up at a moment's notice if called upon. "I do not wish," he continued, "to aggravate the situation by bringing in free labour, and shall not do so unless in the direst circumstances."

Rumours that the coalowners had brought in stokers from Cardiff Docks to help to keep the pumps and ventilation systems working, greatly angered the strikers and intensified the conflict. 'Blacklegs' were brought by train straight into the colliery sidings unseen by the pickets. In some instances the strikers stopped trains to search for stokers coming up from Cardiff and took over a signal box at Llwynypia for the same purpose, until police took control.

Confrontation: Monday 7th November 1910

On Monday, 7th November 1910, a week after the official strike had begun, the confrontation took a new form. Early that morning, colliers and their families in the Tonypandy area were called to action by the sound of a bugle. In the darkness, thousands assembled to march to their neighbouring colliery with the intention of raking out the boiler fires, and stopping any men from doing work at the collieries.

Pickets took up positions at street corners, with the main body of men congregating at the entrances of the various collieries under the control of the Combine. The organisation was extremely effective making it practically impossible for any man to get to work unobserved. Those workmen and officials who attempted to get to work found an impassable barrier of bodies formed by the men closing up together. Some workmen were hustled and others were frog-marched back home.

The local paper graphically described the scene,

"Immediately an engineman or stoker made an appearance, a cry of "Stop him!" was generally raised by the pickets.....In this way man after man was turned back, and so effective was the picketing that, not with-standing the darkness of the early morning, hardly anyone escaped the vigilant eyes of the men who were on the look-out."
The Rhondda Leader, November 1910

So effective was the picketing that later in the day strikers forced their way into the buildings at the Cambrian Colliery Clydach Vale and succeeded in raking out the boiler fires and stopping the ventilating fans. Heavy stoning of the windows of the Powerhouse forced officials to abandon the building and all work ceased. Throughout the Mid-Rhondda district similar actions were successful in closing down all collieries except one.

The one colliery that continued to function was the Glamorgan Colliery, Llwynypia.

Later that day a meeting of the miners was held at the Mid-Rhondda Athletic ground. Several thousand men then marched peacefully to picket at the Glamorgan Colliery. A small group of youths broke away from the marchers to climb the embankment opposite the entrance to the colliery, from where they stoned the police guarding the gateway. Stones were also thrown at the Powerhouse shattering all its windows, resulting in Leonard Llewellyn complaining to the Chief Constable that it was impossible for his men to continue working within the building.

The Chief Constable ordered his men to draw their batons and to charge the crowd. Serious hand to hand fighting took place and continued until midnight, before the police were able to clear the roadway as far as Tonypandy town square, a quarter of a mile away. Wooden palings surrounding the colliery were ripped down, exposing the Powerhouse and the colliery pay office was attacked and wrecked. The Chief Constable, Colonel Lionel Lindsay, was alarmed by the events of that evening. He feared that the police would not be able to repel further attacks. As a result at 1.00am on Tuesday 8th November, he telegraphed the army for troops to be sent to Tonypandy.

RIOTS IN MID-RHONDDA.

Collieries Seized by the Strikers.

Boiler Fires Raked Out.

Craftsmen Chased and Cornered

Police Attack Crowd with Truncheons.

Scenes unparalleled in its history occurred at Mid-Rhondda on Monday, and incidents of violence to persons and property were numerous.

Pickets were posted at every street corner and at every entrance to the various collieries owned by the Combine, while processions of men and women

Mounted Police Stoned.

The mounted police were a special object of hostility. Several horses were nearly carried off their feet by the men's rushes, and stones, tin cans, &c., were thrown at the officers. At Clydach Vale, one of the policemen was struck by a bucket which was used by a woman

How 'The Rhondda Leader' reported it

7th November 1910

The afternoon of Monday 7th November 1910. Thousands of strikers from throughout the area picket outside the Glamorgan colliery where the machinery in the Powerhouse continued to operate despite earlier picketing. Two miners wear shrouds and carry a placard with a warning to strike breakers.

Confrontation **Police Guard The Entrance to The Cambrian Colliery**

Policemen guard the entrance to the Cambrian Collieries Clydach Vale, but were unable to prevent the mass picketing forcing it to close down

Confrontation The March to The Cambrian Colliery 7th November 1910

Early morning on Monday 7th November. Miners and their families marched to their local colliery to prevent any workmen entering the premises

Confrontation **Families Support Strikers Outside The Cambrian Colliery**

Confrontation **Picket Duties**

Pickets wearing their union badges on duty outside a colliery premises on a cold November day 1910. Inset pickets watch from a mountainside vantage point for any workman or official attempting to go to work

63

Confrontation Strikers at Entrance to The Glamorgan Colliery Monday 7th November

Another one of a remarkable series of photographs used in the book taken by local photographer Levi Ladd.

He succeeded in having total control of the crowd of miners just before the rioting started ... the lamp light is still intact!

EASTER HOLIDAYS.

L. LADD, Photographic Artist,

21, Dunraven Street, TONYPANDY.

Wishes to inform his numerous customers and the Public generally that his Studio will be

OPEN ON GOOD FRIDAY

And during the Holidays,

When an opportunity offers itself to families, parties, etc., to be Photographed.

Photography Right up-to-date in all its Branches.

The Oldest Established in the District. Special Quotations for Sunday School and other Groups.

Note Only Address—Opposite Danix's Temperance Bar, and next door to Oliver's Boot Shop.

4788

Confrontation **The Glamorgan Colliery**

EYE WITNESS: Sarah Ann Jones and Margaret Williams witnessed the first night of rioting outside the Glamorgan Colliery on Monday 7th November

"After my mother and father returned from Salem Chapel in the evening around 8.15pm they told us about the happenings outside the colliery. My Aunt said, 'lets go down and see Sarah Ann,' so down we went, my Aunt with baby in arms."

"I used to say to my daughter, 'Well, you're lucky to be alive. It's a wonder you, me, and Auntie Nan weren't killed that night.'

When we got down to the colliery we stood in row with the policemen who were in two rows across the colliery entrance. The miners were up on the bank where they had gathered piles of stones - it was a prepared thing. There was lots of shouting from up on the bank but you couldn't understand what was being said because there was so much noise. The miners shouted to me, 'Get from there with that baby missus.' As we left the police, the stones began to fly, we could hear them as we made our way home. The police there were Glamorgans and Bristol."

Miners crowd around the heavily guarded entrance to the Glamorgan Colliery

Confrontation **Attack on the Powerhouse**

Damage from stone throwing to the Powerhouse at the Glamorgan colliery. These attacks were aimed at disrupting the work of officials operating the machinery which controlled the water pumps and ventilation systems underground

Confrontation Aftermath of Rioting at Glamorgan Colliery

The 'morning after'. The scene outside the Glamorgan Colliery on Tuesday 8th November after the previous days serious fighting between the police and the miners

Confrontation Aftermath of Rioting at Glamorgan Colliery

The photograph from the front page of a national newspaper showing the damage outside the colliery. The photo of William Stanton, a colourful miners leader from Aberdare, has been superimposed (Stanton was not involved in the events outside the Powerhouse!)

Another view of the scenes outside of the Glamorgan Colliery on the morning of the 8th November

The wooden palings surrounding the perimeter of the colliery have been ripped up and used by the strikers as obstacles to the charges of the mounted police.

The picture show the Powerhouse completely exposed and the pay office wrecked.

EYE WITNESS: A striker describes the tactics used on the second night of rioting 8th November 1910
"We congregated again next night but were prepared for them now, we had pulled the wooden stakes off, that is a wall around the colliery, a wooden fence with spike stakes. We pulled them but prior to that we had barrelled stones ready there, we took them off the colliery there ....we had barrelled stones ready there - Well we pre-arranged this and sent the boys up now to irritate the police." Coal hewer, John Wannell

Confrontation Police Guard The Glamorgan Colliery

EYE WITNESS: PC KNIPE

"Yes, yes they were trying to get into the colliery premises to wreck the colliery premises. We had a terrible job driving them back to the Square. It was that night then that they wrecked all the shops. There they were then, parading about there, white waistcoats, top hats and God knows what, like a lot of show men."

'Fortress Glamorgan' where police guard the colliery premises on a wet November day!

Confrontation Tuesday 8th November 1910

Fierce fighting between police and strikers occurred during the evening of Monday, 7th November and lasted until the early hours of Tuesday 8th. The Chief Constable Lionel Lindsay fearful that his men would lose control of the situation, communicated directly with the military authority at Tidworth, Salisbury Plain, to request both infantry and cavalry support. Haldane, Secretary of State for War, organised the despatch of troops and cavalry. Winston Churchill on hearing this at 10am countermanded the order, stopping the infantry at Swindon and the cavalry at Cardiff. This was done either to avoid escalating an already tense situation or to act as a veiled threat of the use of the military. The Chief Constable was then informed of the new arrangements involving the despatch of 70 mounted and 200 foot constables of the Metropolitan Police instead.

At noon on the 8th November a mass meeting of miners was held at the Athletic Ground, Tonypandy, at which a message from Winston Churchill, was read out. It was contained in a telegram to the Chief Constable.

> *"You may give the miners the following message from me:- Their best friends here are greatly distressed at the trouble which has broken out and will do their best to help them to get fair treatment. Askwith, Board of Trade, wishes to see Mr. Watts Morgan with six or eight local representatives at Board of Trade, 2 o'clock tomorrow. But rioting must cease at once so that the enquiry shall not be prejudiced and to prevent the credit of the Rhondda Valley being injured. Confiding in the good sense of the Cambrian Combine workmen we are holding back the soldiers for the present and sending only police."*

The message was well received and the meeting broke up in an orderly manner. A procession of several thousand men then formed and headed towards the Glamorgan Colliery. For some time after arriving there the situation was peaceful, but around 5.00pm some youths started throwing stones at the Powerhouse and within a very short time had succeeded in breaking every window pane facing the roadway. The shattering of the glass made work inside the Powerhouse impossible and this news was conveyed to the Chief Constable who gave the order for his mounted police to charge to clear the gateway. This was done, but with much difficulty as some of the miners, armed with mandril shafts, pickaxes and iron bars fought ferociously. When the officers returned to the entrance, they were further bombarded with a barrage of stones thrown from the high bank opposite the main entrance, resulting in more injuries. Meanwhile, mounted constables were cut off near Llwynypia Post Office and had to be rescued by a detachment of foot police, who then cleared the high bank opposite the colliery entrance.

After a short respite, Lindsay ordered the mounted police to clear the road to Tonypandy, while a body of foot police cleared the road to Llwynypia in the other direction. After hard fighting, in which the Chief Constable was himself injured, the strikers were driven away some distance from the colliery, but they soon returned to their original positions. After several charges, the police, who by now, were exhausted, decided on one last charge to break the strikers' spirit. 80 to 90 constables charged from the colliery cutting a way through the crowd, then, dividing into two sections drove the rioters to Llwynypia and down the road to Tonypandy.

The battle lasted for over two hours during which time further parts of the perimeter fencing of large wooden palings were demolished by the miners. They were to be strewn in the roadway as a barrier to charges by the mounted policemen. Scores of men on both sides were injured, many from head wounds. A miner Samuel Rays died in the battle from skull injuries. At his inquest it was stated that he died as a result of blows from a blunt instrument.

From 8pm the town of Tonypandy, now without any police presence, was in the hands of the strikers and an orgy of window smashing and looting of business premises along the whole length of the town took place.

At 10 pm, the first contingent of Metropolitan Police arrived and, looking to neither right nor left marched through the town. Eventually they turned into the Skating Rink to be sworn in by local magistrates. Now, with legal powers of arrest, they cleared the streets rapidly, without need to use their batons, ordering those who lingered to get off home.

After the night of violence, the police were forced to send for 300 batons to replace those broken or lost in the battle. However, a policeman commented a baton was no match against a mandril handle.

Confrontation Tuesday 8th November 1910

A large crowd of miners gather for the second day outside the entrance to the Glamorgan Colliery on the afternoon of Tuesday, 8th November 1910. In the background a group of strikers surround an official who has to be rescued by the police

Confrontation Violent Scenes Outside The Glamorgan Colliery

General Macready in a report to the Home Office on the 4th December 1910 reflected on the causes of the violent confrontation at the Glamorgan Colliery, *"the violent action of the mob was due to Marxian teachings of local socialists, The attack on Llwynypia on Monday 7th November, was the direct outcome of a Socialist meeting, which was held the previous day, at which the creed of Malatesta, the Spanish anarchist, was preached.*

The mob was thoroughly worked up and in Clem Edward's (Liberal MP) opinion would, the following day have wrecked the Power station, if access had been gained."

CAVALRY SENT FOR.

We understand that 100 cavalry and 200 infantry have been ordered by Captain Lindsay from Salisbury Plain. They will arrive at Llwynypia Station to-day.

It is believed that some of the 18th (Queen Mary's Own) Hussars will be sent to the disturbed districts. This regiment is at present stationed at Tidworth, Salisbury Plain, and could entrain at a moment's notice, as complete troop trains, with the steam up, are awaiting orders at Ludgershall.

The Glamorgan Colliery had a huge perimeter of over two miles long which made it very difficult to defend. Police and soldiers focussed on guarding the main entrance to the colliery and the buildings containing the boilers and the electrical generators.

Tents were erected on the forecourt to provide shelter for the occupying police force.

Confrontation The Consequences

On the evening of Tuesday 8th November 40 policemen from the Bristol, Cardiff, Swansea and Glamorgan forces (including 16 mounted) were injured in the disturbances outside the Glamorgan colliery or on the road into Tonypandy. The Chief Constable of Glamorgan Lionel Lindsay is listed as having an 'injury to the right leg and hand' whilst the Deputy Constable Cole had injuries 'to the chin and right in step'.

204 police injuries resulted from clashes in the Mid-Rhondda area In the months from November 1910 to July 1911.

Serious clashes occurred on the 7th and 8th November at Llwynypia and Tonypandy and on the 21st at Penygraig.

In 1911 there were ugly disturbances on 22nd and 23rd at Clydach Vale and at Blaenclydach and on the 4th May at Blaenclydach and Tonypandy. The final confrontation took place at the Ely colliery on 25th July 1911. Over 500 minor injuries were not recorded.

An injured Cardiff policeman showing the 'Mets' where a stone had struck his helmet. Most injuries to policemen resulted from stone throwing

EYE WITNESS: P.C. Davies of the Swansea Police contingent which was drafted in to support the Glamorgan police, was injured in the confrontation outside the Glamorgan Colliery, he described what happened:

"The strikers were stoning from a high bank outside the Glamorgan Colliery when the order came to charge. We went up the bank baton in hand, and as I was running, I was struck on the ankle by a stone, and I fell to the ground helpless. Two or three fell on top of me, and I did not regain consciousness till nearly 7.30pm last night.

I have never seen anything like it in my life. It was terrible. There was blood everywhere, and injured men were lying about all over the place. Even the women had their aprons full of stones. The Swansea men were in the thick of it, the two Mills, and Skinner all had cuts on their heads."

Using stones, hammers and iron bars, the strikers moved forward ... and the police defended

Confrontation The Aftermath

EYE WITNESS: Lilly Pontsford remembers the first night of the rioting

"Arthur and I were going home one night from the 'pictures'. From the old 'Hip'.

…and as we got up to the colliery the tramcar came down from by Parry the Post Office. It had to come down and it got in the middle of the men. One lot of men rushed one way and a lot rushed the other, watching for 'blacklegs', that they weren't going to work.

…and the police must have thought they were rushing to them, so the inspector called "Charge!", and of course the police scattered the men all ways, from the tramcar to come through see. And then we all had to run. The police on horseback was charging the men and the police on foot, and attacking the people. The inspector called "Charge!" and that started it. Believe me, I've never run so much in my life.

And we, we run up there and Arthur, I don't know where Arthur went, but I ran like the devil.,… and I run and we run in houses. In Mrs Davies', in Grange Terrace. Yes, I run in there out of the way. And then after everything, when I thought was quiet, I went now to go home. I lived in Partridge Road.

I went through the terraces now and down the hill by Llwynypia Station, by those little huts at the bottom. Just on the side of Parry the Post there.

As I came out on the road, Mrs Parry was on the road asking people if they would come in and help bathe the men's wounds. So what I done, instead of going home I went in there see.

(It was) about ten o'clock, because we weren't allowed out late at night. Young girls wasn't then. We had to be home nine o'clock, half past nine. So I went in there, … I was in there close on three o'clock in the morning.

…there was ever such a lot, men and young boys, and they were hit about all shapes, … beaten with the truncheons. And I'll say this for Mrs Parry mind, she ripped up all sorts of cloths, sheets and things, to bandage those men. And she'd made them cups of tea and tried to put them as comfortable as they could, until they were fit to go home.

…there was lots came in Parry the Post, it was through the back, not through the Post Office. She's got a back yard like, take them around that way into her kitchen, … it was about three,.in the morning, when I went home. Yes, because my mother and father were petrified."

2 miners with patched up scalp wounds talking about their experiences

"The Cavalry arrived at mid-day and are encamped quite near to the school. Consequently there has been added a still further cause for non-attendance at school of pupils who live near the school. Mr. Griffiths one of our Assistant Masters was truncheoned last night in one of their charges along the thoroughfare. Many innocent pedestrians suffered from police charges."

Headmaster Llwynypia primary school (School Log Book entry) 9th November, 1910

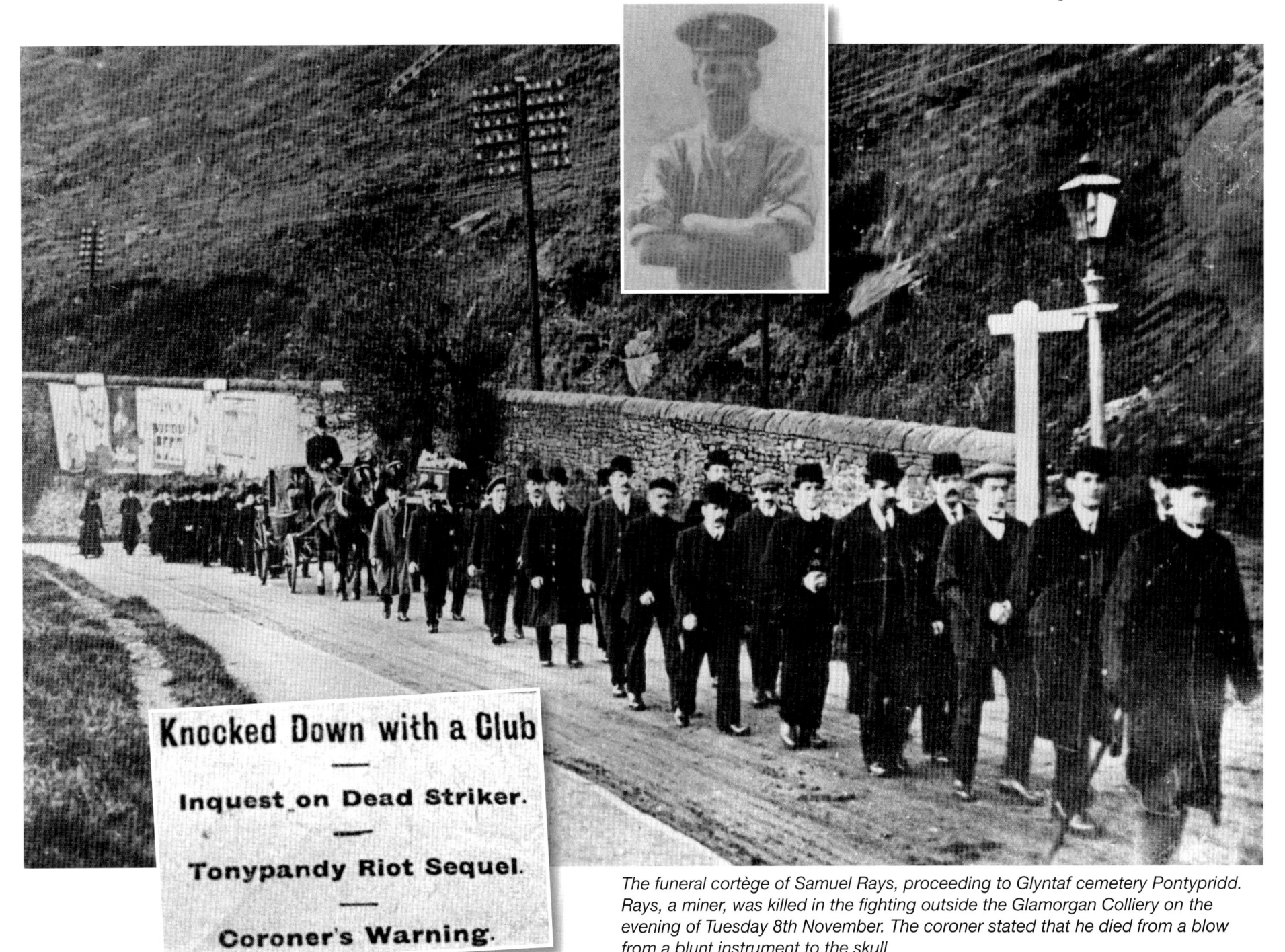

Confrontation **The Consequences: The Death of a Miner**

Knocked Down with a Club

Inquest on Dead Striker.

Tonypandy Riot Sequel.

Coroner's Warning.

The funeral cortège of Samuel Rays, proceeding to Glyntaf cemetery Pontypridd. Rays, a miner, was killed in the fighting outside the Glamorgan Colliery on the evening of Tuesday 8th November. The coroner stated that he died from a blow from a blunt instrument to the skull

The Looting of Tonypandy: Who and Why?

The rioting and looting of the town of Tonypandy during the evening of Tuesday 8th November 1910 resulted in considerable press coverage both nationally and Internationally.

Late on that Tuesday afternoon serious rioting had again occurred outside the Glamorgan Colliery. Hand to hand fighting took place, until the police were able to drive the crowd away from the entrance of the colliery in the direction of Tonypandy town centre.

What happened next has been subject of much debate ever since. What we do know is that a 'crowd' attacked and looted the shops in Tonypandy, For three hours the main street of Tonypandy was given up to looting and rioting. Shop fronts were smashed and the contents thrown into the street. Goods of all description drapery, millinery, grocery provisions littered the streets. Looters carried away rolls of cloth, hats, umbrellas, bundles of clothing and even shop fittings. Hayden Jones shop on Pandy Square suffered the most damage - losing over £1,200 of stock. Over 60 shops were looted, however, a chemists shop belonging to local hero Willie Llewellyn the Welsh rugby international was left untouched

National newspapers had headlines such as 'Ruse that failed'; and 'Town wrecked to lure police from the Colliery' interpreted the events as one of striking miners attacking their own town to try to divert the police from the nearby Glamorgan Colliery. Others suggested that they were caused by the strikers frustration having failed to take control of the Powerhouse.

General Macready, who was placed in charge of the military by Winston Churchill, did not agree with the newspapers' accounts. He offered a realistic assessment of the situation stating that had the crowd of over 9,000 miners wanted to invade the colliery premises there would have been little that the police could have done to prevent it as the colliery area was too large to be completely protected.

Debate raged over who was responsible for the damage and looting of the shops. Church leaders wrote to the press defending the reputation of their community. In Parliament Keir Hardie, M.P. for Merthyr and Aberdare, stated that had there been half dozen policemen on duty on the streets of Tonypandy the rioting and looting would not have happened and that the number of men taking part in the window smashing never exceeded a hundred.

In recent years historian Dai Smith has suggested that there was underlying resentment towards members of the shopping community which can help to explain the rioting and looting of the town. Some shopkeepers owned and rented many houses and expected their tenants to buy at their shops. There was a close relationship between the general manager and leading members of the shop owners through the Chamber of Trade and attendance at the local church. Rumours also circulated that certain shopkeepers had made remarks which were less than sympathetic towards the miners' cause.

Views from the Time

From a book written in 1912 a year after the strike 'Labour Strife in the South Wales Coalfield 1910-11' - David Evans
'Immediately after the repulse of the attack on the Glamorgan colliery came the sack of Tonypandy ...In their flight from Llwynypia and under the impression that the victorious police were still at their heels, the rioters desperate at the defeat of their plans to take the colliery, gave vent to their rage by smashing windows of every shop that came within reach.'

A letter to 'The Times' from the vicar of Llwynypia and two nonconformist ministers
'Sir, The press reports covering street rioting and shop looting in Tonypandy and Llwynypia have given the reading public the impression that it was carried out by the general body of strikers, whereas the plain truth is that it was the work of a certain small gang of half drunken, irresponsible persons, many, if not the majority of whom were from outside the affected district. Earlier in the day, at a mass meeting of the workmen at which the stipendiary of our district received a hearty welcome, all the leaders strongly deprecated any form of violence. This advice was received with applause by all, and they marched in a body of 10,000 strong, without causing the slightest disturbance.'

The view of General Macready the Military Commander
'Desperate attempts' to sack the Powerhouse at Llwynypia proved to have been an attempt to force the gateway,... and a good deal of stone throwing... and had the mob been as numerous or so determined as the reports implied, there was nothing to have prevented them from over running the whole premises.' From 'Annals of an Active Life'

of TONYPANDY

The Looting of Tonypandy The Day After

Pandy Square the morning of 9th November 1910

Miners and their families survey the devastation

Philips the draper's wrecked shop

EYE WITNESS: Thomas Bartlett
"My father said to me, 'Mind you walk in the middle of the road, and don't stop for anyone'.

As we walked over the bridge, a crowd came rushing down the road, shouting 'Police! Police!' and we could see the police with batons drawn in full pursuit. My father said "Keep by me and don't do anything."

As we got to Pandy Square, the place was thronged with people.

One fellow who recognized my father shouted to him to 'come over and join in the fun.'

My father replied, 'No, no, we're going home straight'.

Just then, a tin of salmon came flying past my ear into Haydn Jones' window."

The Looting of Tonypandy **The Day After**

A stunned crowd on Pandy Square the day after the rioting and looting

A shopkeeper boards up the smashed glass frontage of his premises, the morning after the rioting and looting of the town of Tonypandy

The Looting of Tonypandy 'Zinc City'

The boarded shop windows which led commentators to refer to Tonypandy as 'Zinc City'. Only 2 shops remained undamaged. A jewellers owned by Barney Issac which had shutters to protect its windows and a chemists shop owned by Willie Llewellyn (properties on the far right). Llewellyn was a Welsh rugby international who had played in the team which defeated the 'invincible' All Blacks in 1905. He also scored 4 tries in an international match against England. In the photograph Llewellyn's shop is also boarded which may have been done for protection the day after the rioting

The Looting of Tonypandy **J. Owen Jones Draper**

A scene near Tonypandy Square on the morning of Wednesday, 9th November. The draper's shop owned by J. Owen Jones is completely boarded, having been ransacked during the previous evening's rioting

The Looting of Tonypandy J. Owen Jones Draper

Mid-Rhondda Chamber of Trade 1909
Bottom left President Leonard Llewellyn, bottom right Chairman J. Owen Jones draper

Police Accommodation at the Rink.

Proprietors Had No Option.

The proprietors of the Pavilion Skating Rink, Tonypandy, which has been commandeered by order of the magistrates for the accommodation of the Metropolitan Police, have been subjected to much abuse and insolence by a section of the strikers, who maintain that these local gentlemen are assisting the authorities as against the men. Mr. John Jones, the father of one of the proprietors, was severely handled by a gang of roughs on Tuesday, and narrowly escaped a severe beating.

It is unnecessary to point out that the Rink proprietors had no option in the matter, as the following communication will show:—

To the Proprietors and Manager, Tonypandy Skating Rink.

I hereby request and order you to hand over the Skating Rink premises to the Police Authorities for the purpose of accommodating His Majesty's troops called in to suppress riots under the Riot Act.

D. LLEUFER THOMAS,
Stipendiary Magistrate.
8th November, 1910.

The Jones family owned the Skating Rink in Tonypandy which was commandeered for use as accommodation for hundreds of Metropolitan police sent to the area

J. Owen Jones, a draper, was a prominent member of the local establishment.

He was Chairman of the Mid-Rhondda Chamber of Trade and had close associations with Leonard Llewellyn the General Manager of the Cambrian Collieries. The Skating Rink, which he owned, was used to accommodate the police drafted into the area.

Rumours abounded that he had made a disparaging remark about the miner's decision to strike. *'half a loaf is good enough for a miner'*. Jones denied the accusation and after his shop was ransacked inserted a notice in the local newspaper offering a reward of £50 (a considerable sum of money in 1910).

£50 Reward.

I, J. Owen Jones, draper, Tonypandy, offer a reward of £50 to the Cambrian Combine Committee, to be given by them to any charity or charities they may choose, if a certain statement attributed to me can be proved correct.

Dated this 10th day of November, 1910.

J. OWEN JONES.

A notice displayed in 'The Rhondda Leader' 12th November and subsequent editions following the rioting and looting of the shops on the 8th November 1910

The Looting of Tonypandy J. Owen Jones Draper

J. Owen Jones advertised extensively to attract customers. Earlier in the summer of 1910 he had invited customers to view and purchase some of the large back-log of stock he wished to clear.

Looters removed over £1,000 of stock

Hostility towards Shopkeepers
"By some it is stated to have been refusal on the part of a tradesman to accommodate two men who had been injured, and by others a taunt directed against a number of strikers by a shopkeeper who had the reputation of having consistently condemned the actions of the Cambrian and Glamorgan miners in coming out on strike."
The Morning Post

EYE WITNESS: Gwen Cunningham, a maid servant at Glyncornel saw the looting on her way home that evening
"...they broke Owen Jones' window to pieces. There was a man called, ... he was in there and he had six or seven bowler hats on his head and a roll of cloth under his arm and a packet of stockings under the other arm coming out from there and there they were then, all of them. Each one had a parcel of some description, ... he passed me and he was carrying all that junk home. Well then they went down, lower down, and they were breaking all the shops up, Now they were getting desperate.
  ... Oilcloth, everything. You know, they've got rolls of cloth. Cloths under their arms, trousers, everything, and oilcloth and bowler hats and blouses and God knows what.
  I was there for hours. I couldn't get away from there. You couldn't move see."

An advert in The Rhondda Leader 1910

Have you been in yet?

If not, you should lose no time. The Bargains I am offering this year at my **WINTER SALE** are far and away ahead of what I have ever been able to offer before.

It has been a most peculiar season; the one just passed was a season of surprises. The most unlikely things have happened. Goods that I made sure would be entirely cleared out long ago are still here, but they are only here for a very short time.

The red ink has been hard at work, and regardless of values, prices have been cut, and it only remains for you to pay an early visit for you to be able to secure goods of sterling merit and worth at a mere fraction of what they would have fetched, had weather conditions been normal. So that taken altogether my **WINTER SALE** will be a veritable time of bargain securing for those who are fortunate enough to participate—be sure you are among the number.

Owing to Pending Structural Alterations
I shall be unable to display all bargains in the windows for at least one week. If my patrons do not see what they require in the windows, will they kindly do me a favour by stepping inside and stating their requirements when they will receive the utmost attention.

J. OWEN JONES, Draper etc.,
Pandy Square, **TONYPANDY.**

The Looting Of Tonypandy Traders' Complaints

The almost deserted town of Tonypandy, on a wet November day, a few days after the rioting and looting

'The town was entirely at the mercy of the crowd, and the town on Wednesday morning resembled a besieged town. The shop windows all along De Winton and Dunraven Streets were barricaded, and tradesmen stood gloomily in their doorways amidst the terrible wreckage around them. Nothing like it has ever been seen in South Wales.'
Rhondda Leader – November 1910

Traders' Bitter Complaint
'Local traders are complaining bitterly because the streets were left totally unguarded on Tuesday night. All the police force, they say, being concentrated in protecting the collieries.'
Rhondda Leader

The Looting of Tonypandy 'We Saw It Happen'

EYE WITNESS: Annie Mary Thurston lived in Dunraven Street Tonypandy and witnessed the rioting and looting on Tuesday, 8th November,

"At Llwynypia, and my brother was also a miner, and they both worked in Llwynypia Colliery, isn't it…… We were expecting some kind of bother for quite a while. My father tried to keep us in, in the evenings, and that because they were saying that there was going to be some kind of an upset. Well, the night of the riots we were all at home and we could hear this terrible noise coming down from the very top of the street.

It was about half past seven to eight, if I can remember rightly, and they came down, and a lot of men on one side… …each side of the road. There was two lots of men carrying these different implements with them, and as they were coming down the street they were smashing the windows each side as they were coming.

This carried on and down the road they were smashing the windows. They were looting as they were smashing. People coming down and looting every shop."

EYE WITNESS: Edith Hancock resident of Williamstown, Her brothers were Glamorgan policemen drafted into the district.

"Well, I went to look for two of my brothers that was up in the skating rink, to the Glamorgan police that had been drafted in. I didn't find them of course and I dawdled about the place and all of a sudden here's the smashing going to start and we were all rushed in to Danix's Temperance Bar

When you came out you could hear the glass and that, the glass still falling about see. Of course we went down then and we were told to go home, and pretty severely told to go home see. For I was a very small sixteen,. Well we were told then, police it must have been, because I said I wanted to see my brothers, I dawdled to see my brothers, But you mustn't stop! You've got to go home!"

EYE WITNESS: William Henry, Lewis a miner on strike

"I saw them looting everything, people were coming out of shops with suits and shoes in boxes.

One man came out from a shop carrying a big American cheese weighing about 30-40 lbs. and he had a side of bacon.

I said to him, 'Where are you going butty?'

He replied ' Gilfach - where do you think'."

The Looting of Tonypandy What The Papers Said

DAILY SKETCH

THURSDAY, NOVEMBER 10, 1910. THE PREMIER PICTURE PAPER. ONE HALFPENNY

WELSH TOWN WRECKED BY STRIKE RIOTERS.

The events at Tonypandy, particularly after the rioting and looting of the town on the 8th November featured as headlines in newspapers in Britain and across the world

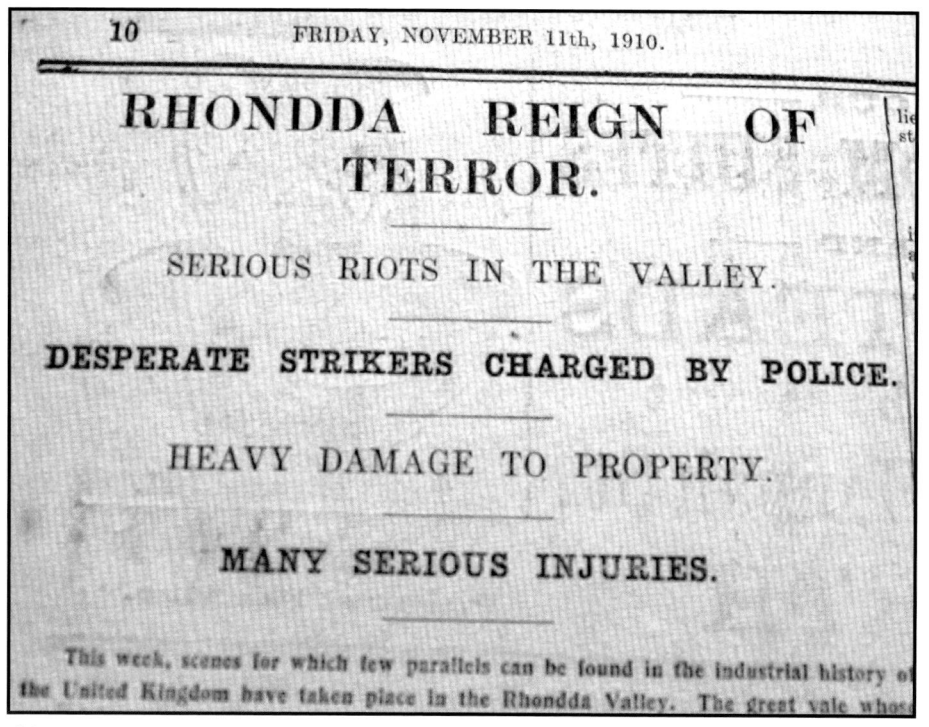

FRIDAY, NOVEMBER 11th, 1910.

RHONDDA REIGN OF TERROR.

SERIOUS RIOTS IN THE VALLEY.

DESPERATE STRIKERS CHARGED BY POLICE.

HEAVY DAMAGE TO PROPERTY.

MANY SERIOUS INJURIES.

This week, scenes for which few parallels can be found in the industrial history of the United Kingdom have taken place in the Rhondda Valley.

Glamorgan Free Press, 11th November 1910

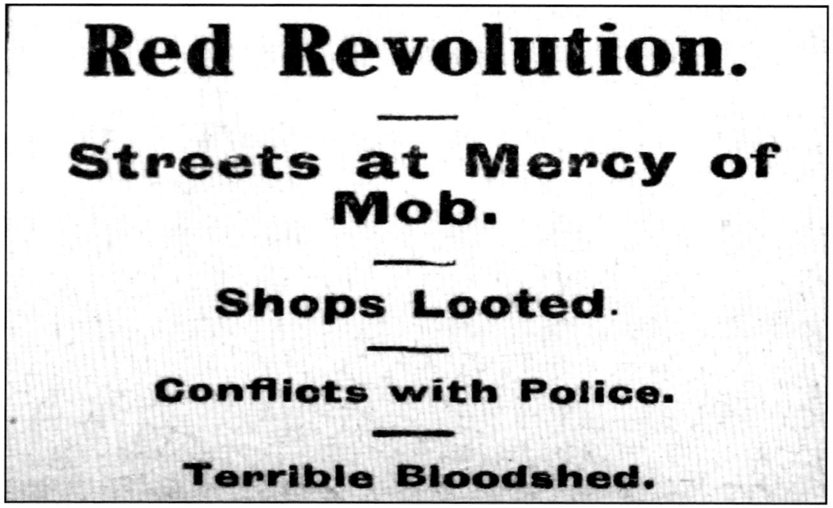

Red Revolution.

Streets at Mercy of Mob.

Shops Looted.

Conflicts with Police.

Terrible Bloodshed.

How the local newspaper 'The Rhondda Leader' saw it

Two reports from General Macready, which show his concern about the impact of provocative press reports. The first was sent to Churchill on 18th November 1910 and the second dated 11th January 1911.

'Alarmist paragraph about explosives. Mr. Lawrence secretary to Llewellyn denied he had given information, I know that he is in constant communication with reporters and pointed out that if he continued to be the cause of reports calculated to alarm inhabitants and increase cause of unrest I should take steps to remove him from the district, Churchill replied *'We are bound by civil law and we have no power to remove objectionable persons from the strike area'*

January 1911 *'It is as well to mention that one of the factors, that has tended to inflame men's minds and keep up the agitation has been the sensational and inaccurate reports in the local press. In one case the confidential secretary to a manager had formerly been a press reporter, and I was obliged to take both him and his employer severely to task for the exaggerated press reports of which he was the instigator. The strikers fully recognised the baneful effect of the local press, to such an extent that on at least one occasion reporters who attempted to attend a meeting were roughly handled.'*

The Role of Winston Churchill: The Churchill Controversy

The role of Winston Churchill in the events of Tonypandy in 1910 and their outcome, had major political repercussions both at the time and far beyond those years. It became a bitter issue in the general election of 1950 and after his death, in a heated parliamentary debate in 1978. In 1910 Winston Churchill was the Home Secretary in Asquith's Liberal government. One of his responsibilities was to deal with situations of civil disorder.

The disturbances outside the Glamorgan colliery, Llwynypia, on the evening of Monday 7th November, had resulted in many casualties to both workmen and the police. The Chief Constable of Glamorgan, Lionel Lindsay, had considered his contingents of policemen insufficient to combat the violence and had directly contacted the army for the support of two companies of soldiers.

At first the Home Secretary countermanded the order and halted the infantry at Swindon and the cavalry at Cardiff. He responded to the Chief Constable's request by sending reinforcements of several hundred Metropolitan policemen. However, a further serious disturbance outside the Glamorgan Colliery on the evening of the 8th November and the 'sacking' of the town of Tonypandy resulted in appeals from both the Chief Constable and the Stipendiary Magistrate for military support. This was authorised by Churchill and a squadron of the 18th Hussars rode into Tonypandy at mid-day on the 9th November.

Churchill sent to the valleys nearly 1,000 Metropolitan police, several regiments of infantry and mounted troops.

They remained throughout the winter of 1910 until early summer of 1911.

Some historians have argued that Churchill's initial response in holding back the military was due to the weakness of the Liberal Party electorally. A second General Election was due in December 1910 and the Liberal party needed the support of mining communities like the Rhondda. The Liberal Party in 1910 remained in power due to the support of other parties, and any action against the Rhondda mining community could lead to the withdrawal of support by both Liberal and Labour members across England and Wales.

It has also been suggested that Churchill was mindful of the events of the 'Featherstone Shootings' when the then Home Secretary Asquith (now the Liberal Prime Minister) ordered the military into action in that area of Yorkshire with the result that workers were shot. What is certain is that the use of the military resulted in fierce criticism of Churchill in the national and local press and in Parliament.

He was condemned by the coal owners and by the Conservative press for weakness in holding back troops, whilst labour leaders including Keir Hardie M.P. condemned the Home Secretary's authorization of the use of the military as being totally unnecessary and offensive to the law-abiding people in the coal communities. Tonypandy remained as one of the black spots of Churchill's political career.

> I have told General Macready to proceed to Tonypandy to-night to support you. You will, I am sure, work with him with the utmost cordiality. Please express to the police officers under your charge, particularly those who bore the strain yesterday, my appreciation of the courage, discipline and good spirit which they have shown throughout these troubles. Their fine qualities are the only means of averting the employment of the military. You should proclaim throughout the town that all wellmeaning citizens should remain in their homes tonight, and that sight-seers expose themselves to considerable risks by mingling with the crowd. If you can spare the time telegraph how you have distributed the police forces at your disposal. Unless you have more serious calls elsewhere you should use the whole of the third contingent of three hundred metropolitan police in Tonypandy tonight and establish a decisive superiority once and for all. Winston Churchill.
>
> (copy of telegram sent to Chief Constable about 5.30 p.m. on Wed. Nov. 9th)

Churchill's telegram to the Chief Constable Lionel Lindsay, Wednesday, 9th November 1910

The ROLE of WINSTON CHURCHILL

The Role of Winston Churchill Arrival of The Military

The Churchill telegram to General Macready authorising the use of the military

The presence of the military ensured that the strikers would be unable to pursue effectively their policy of stopping men, including officials from working.

The military were used in a support role to the police particularly during the trials of miners. Several regiments were involved at different times throughout the 10 month strike: the '18th Hussars', the Lancashire Fusiliers, the Somerset Light Infantry, the Devonshires, the West Ridings and the Royal Munster Fusiliers.

Tuesday 8th NOVEMBER 1910

12.00am	Strikers gather at Tonypandy Square.
1.00am	Police baton charges on Tonypandy Square (2.00am Square secured).
1.00am	Chief Constable Lionel Lindsay telegraphs military HQ at Salisbury Plain for troops as arranged prior to the strike.
3.30am	Haldane despatched 200 cavalry and 2 companies of infantry.
10.00am	Churchill receives telegram from Chief Constable informing him of troop movements. The Home Secretary meets William Abrahams MP, SWMF President.
11.15am	Churchill holds back infantry at Swindon and informs Chief Constable.
12.00noon	Conference of Churchill and the Secretary for War.
12.30pm	Strikers hold mass meeting at Mid-Rhondda Athletic ground. Addressed by the Stipendiary Magistrate and the Chief Constable. A message from Churchill informs strike leaders that he is sending the 'Mets' and is holding back the troops. Strikers march to the Glamorgan Colliery.
1.30pm	Telegram sent to Chief Constable – Metropolitan Police being sent but cavalry to be moved into the district that evening.
2.00pm	Chief Constable telegraphs Churchill about the mass meeting and problems of accommodating the cavalry. Decision to keep cavalry at Cardiff.
5.00-7.00pm	Serious rioting outside the Glamorgan colliery
7.45pm	Telegram from Stipendiary Magistrate, Lleufer Thomas to Home Office appealing for military to be released from Cardiff for Tonypandy.
8.00pm	Telegram from Home Office to General Macready in charge of military - " Proceed if necessary" (copied to Lindsay).
8.15pm	Smashing and looting of the shops at Tonypandy. Further destruction of perimeter palings of the Glamorgan Colliery.
10.00pm	First Contingent of Metropolitan Police arrive at Tonypandy
10.30pm	First squadron of 18th Hussars arrive at Pontypridd
12.00pm	Police in control of the Tonypandy town.

Wednesday 9th November

12.00noon	18th Hussars arrive at Tonypandy

The timetable of events leading to the use of the military at Tonypandy

The Role of Winston Churchill **Arrival of The Military**

The arrival of the military. The 18th Hussars enter Tonypandy, Wednesday 9th November, 1910

November 9, 1910

HUSSARS ARRIVE

Strikers Attack Collieries and Loot Tonypandy.

SHOPS PLUNDERED.

Mounted and Foot Police Sent from London to South Wales.

MANY INJURED.

Rioters Driven Into Canal by Baton Charges After Fierce Tussle.

MR. CHURCHILL'S ACTION.

The Role of Winston Churchill Arrival of The Military: Their Role

One of the military officers describes the scene as they rode into Tonypandy:

'As we passed through the village of Tonypandy there were signs that serious rioting had taken place. I can honestly say that in France I saw towns and villages evacuated by the Germans which were in better condition than those the rioters had wrecked.

All the shops had been looted, and not only the contents, but the actual fittings (such as gasbrackets, shelves etc.) had been carried off. There was hardly an unbroken pane of glass in the place.

During the rioting in the early evening, when most the damage to property occurred, there were no policemen in the shopping vicinity. All available forces were concentrated at the Glamorgan Colliery defending the Powerhouse. At this stage the forces of law and order were stretched to their very limits. Their absence from the town led to much criticism, for many felt that had there been a small force of constables on the square that evening the orgy of destruction would have been prevented.'

'Episodes and Reflections' by Major-General Sir Wyndham Childs.

Hussars occupy the Glamorgan Colliery buildings

The Role of Winston Churchill **Arrival of The Military: Their Role**

Lancashire Fusiliers guard colliery buildings

Hussars hold back the crowd

During the disturbances the strikers gained advantage over the police by retreating to the mountain side where they could not be caught.

"In order to counter these tactics (of the strikers) small bodies of infantry on the higher ground, keeping level with the police on the main road, moved slowly down the side tracks and by a little gentle persuasion with the bayonet drove the stone throwers into the arms of the police on the lower road."

General Macready illustrates the role of the military

Stipendiary Magistrate Lleufer Thomas discusses matters with the captain of the 18th Hussars

93

The Role of Winston Churchill Who Sent in The Troops?

In response to a question from Keir Hardie MP about who was responsible for sending in the troops, Churchill informed the House that, *"the justices on the spot summoned the military and the military was sent from Southern Command in response to that summons without any reference being made to the Home Office at all. This was brought to my notice, and in consultation with the Secretary of State for War, and in full accordance with his wishes we took the responsibility of arresting the movements of troops, and of going out of ordinary practice to such a point that I prepared with the utmost rapidity a powerful contingent of Metropolitan Police."*

Later in the week he corrected his earlier statement to the House by stating that *"The magistrates I am informed, did not make the requests. The troops were sent directly on the request for assistance by the Chief Constable on the spot."*

The Role of the Chief Constable

Capt. Lionel Lindsay in a letter to O.H.Jones Chairman of the Standing Joint Police Committee dated 5th Nov states,
'If events take a more serious turn I should be compelled to call in 50 cavalry. I do not anticipate having to obtain the aid of the military more especially as I have not come to the end of my police reinforcements yet ... " He also referred to a meeting with magistrates at Pentre, in the Rhondda Valley on 7th November with a view to calling in the military with 50 cavalry being held in readiness at Portsmouth ... he re-iterated his view that he did not anticipate using the military.'

But by 1am on the morning of the **8th November** after serious clashes with the strikers outside the Glamorgan Colliery, Llwynypia, Lindsay telegraphed Haldane at the War Office to despatch troops to the strike area. At 3.30am that morning Haldane despatched 200 cavalry and two companies of infantry from Tidworth for Pontypridd. At 10am, Haldane informed Churchill that the military had left for the strike area.

Churchill stopped the troops at Swindon and sent a telegram to the miners leaders informing them of his action of holding back the troops but sending police reinforcements instead.

The military parade at Park Place Cardiff, on Tuesday 8th November where the troops were held in readiness, awaiting the miners' response to the Home Secretary's telegram asking for a cessation of rioting at Tonypandy.

Churchill did not want to use the military against the civilian population as this could lead to troops opening fire on the strikers. Churchill informed the Commons that he had held back the military *'to avoid the dangers which were inevitable when the military came into collision with a violent mob'.*

He ordered that troops should only be used as a last resort. Their role was however significant in supporting the police throughout the strike ensuring that the miners' tactics were undermined.

Criticism of Churchill ... from All Sides!

Views of the Press

The Delay of Troops will be Deplored

'The sufferers by last night's riot will have a long reckoning with those responsible for the disastrous bungling connected to the despatch of troops. Some ridiculous squeamishness or fear appears to have been allowed to paralyse official action - some recollection, perhaps of the bloodshed of Featherstone when Mr. Asquith was Home Secretary seventeen years ago.'

'South Wales Echo', November, 1910

'To the action of the Home Secretary, Mr. Churchill does not cut a very brilliant figure. To delay compliance with the urgent request of the local authorities for the help of the military was a highly questionable measure, and one that was only likely to encourage the mob to further acts of violence

Nor did Mr. Churchill's whining appeal to the good sense of the strikers produce the slightest effect on restraining them. Pills are a useless prescription for the cure of earthquakes - as Mr. Briand in France has lately had the sense to perceive, but Mr. Churchill, apparently has not.

If the recent disgraceful scenes are not repeated the thanks will be due to the belated arrival of the soldiers on the scene, rather than the Home Secretary's half hearted refusal to look facts in the face with the requisite promptitude and decision.'

Editorial 'Sheffield Telegraph', November 11th, 1910

'The Home Secretary does not shine very brilliantly in his actions with regard to the Welsh strike riots. From his answers given to the House of Commons yesterday, it is clear that Mr. Haldane was prepared to do his duty in providing troops to quell the riots but Mr. Churchill showed he was more concerned about votes than about law and order.'

'York Herald', 16th November, 1910

Views of the Coalowners

"Mr. Winston Churchill's action has really made things worse. I applied for military and saw the magistrates on the Monday morning, and I told them of the seriousness of the case, and my complaint is that none of this bloodshed would have happened if the military had been here.

(Mr. Churchill) asked the representatives of the strikers to come to meet him, and he delayed the troops coming here with the result that the strikers had the idea that these troops are only here for ornament. Mr. Winston Churchill seems to think that there is only one side to this, and I say that he ought to have seen both sides. He spoke as if we were not entitled to any sympathy at all, and it is a significant fact that only when it was discovered that the military were being stopped that the rioting commenced."

Leonard Llewellyn,
General Manager of the Cambrian Combine

"Mr. Churchill made a fatal mistake. I know he had the best intention, but he did not know the desperate character of the men he was dealing with, and his well meant appeals fell on heedless ears. Nay, more, he unwittingly encouraged them to engage in a last desperate riot, while those who could have checked it were not there to do so."

View of a coalowner (a Liberal)

Views of the Miners

"While deeply regretting the disturbances which have occurred, consider that the civil forces are sufficient to deal with such disturbances, and strongly deprecate the employment of the military for such a purpose, and if the military have been sent into the district affected asks the Home Secretary at once to recall them."

Miners' Federation Telegram to Home Office

The Role of Winston Churchill The Use of The Military: Cartoon Interpretations

Better Late than Never. Winston (waking up) Sorry you are having a rough time of it. Now you have my permission to arrest thieves, rioters

Holding Him Back
or how the Home Secretary distinguished himself

DANGEROUS DISEASES NEED DRASTIC REMEDIES

Western Mail cartoons which were critical of Winston Churchill

The Staniforth Cartoons printed in the Western Mail in 1910.

J. M. Staniforth was born in Gloucestershire in 1863 then his family moved to Cardiff where his father kept a shop. He left school at 15 to join the Western Mail as an apprentice printer. His obvious talent for drawing saw him become the cartoonist for that paper and the Evening Express from the late 1880s until his death in 1921.

In 1910 the Western Mail's politically conservative stance led it to be regarded as the coalowner's paper. Staniforth's cartoons from the 1880s to the early 1900s show him to be critical of them yet by 1910 his cartoons portrayed the Mid-Rhondda miners as unreasonable and violent men responsible for events leading to the Cambrian Combine strike.

Law and order were of paramount importance to him. After the looting of Tonypandy on the 8th November, he strongly condemned the failure of Winston Churchill as Home Secretary to provide the military resources early enough as requested by the Chief Constable, Magistrates and the coalowners. His cartoons reflect he and his paper's dislike and fear of the new socialist ideas growing in the valleys.

The Role of Winston Churchill What Did They Really Think? ...

Cambrian Colliery officials 1905

The telegram and memorandum sent during the strike provide useful insights into the attitudes of Churchill and General Macready to the people they had to deal with and contentious issues such as the importation of blackleg labour.

Churchill to General Macready dated 16th November 1910

'I approve your action about electric wires.

You should remember, that the owners are within their legal rights in claiming to import labour but that you are entitled to judge time manner and circumstances of such importation in order that no breach of the peace may be unnecessarily provoked and to ensure that the authorities responsible for keeping order have adequate forces upon the spot. With this leverage you might be able to restrain or at any rate delay injudicious action on part of the owners. I have no powers to veto importation but if you tell me in any particular case it cannot be safely done I shall support you. I have full confidence in your judgement and impartiality and much can be done in these matters by personal influence. Remember however, that we are bound by the civil law and that we have no power to remove objectionable persons from the strike area. Debate in Parliament yesterday was very cool and lifeless and the general impression was that the right thing was being done, You should note my pledge that peaceful picketing will be protected. This, however, does not include trespass which may be dealt with by mine owners but not by police unless it leads or is likely to lead to disorder, Pray consult me on any points which cause you embarrassment.'

General Macready Memorandum to the Home Office about Colliery Managers

'It appeared to me on arriving in this district that a false impression as to the use of both police and military existed in the minds of the managers. There seemed a general idea that the managers were at liberty to carry out any schemes they pleased, such as the importation of "blacklegs", or fresh work on pits, in short any measure without consideration as to how it might influence the strikers, and that the military would then be called upon to support such action. Also there was a distinct inclination to direct and apportion the movements and numbers of both police and military while the information from the managers was in practically every case so exaggerated as to be worthless.'

The Role of Winston Churchill **Arrival of The Military**

The arrival of the Somerset Light Infantry at Tonypandy railway station

The Role of Winston Churchill **Arrival of The Military: Fraternization**

The military take up duties guarding colliery property

EYE WITNESS: John Wannell
"The police didn't mix with people. the soldiers did you know. The first lot of soldiers, the Lancashires they more or less, well mixing with boys, drinking with them, until at last you know,.....if it come too much they send them back home.
... some got married, married the girls here. Well it was commonly known that you could leave Scots terraces houses open in the night…get up in the morning you would find a loaf, a tin of corn beef, perhaps several of them, especially them that was courting the girls living there, They were giving food on the cutie that was mind."

Soldiers Play Football with Strikers
'As showing the good feeling existing between the soldiers now doing duty in the district and the strikers, a football match was played on Tuesday between a team representing the Lancashire Fusiliers and the Mid-Rhondda Athletics. The soldiers trounced their opponents by four goals to one, each of the soldiers goals being heartily cheered.'
'The Rhondda Leader', November, 1910

99

The Role of Winston Churchill The Arrival of The 'Mets'

The 'Mets' are sworn in at Tonypandy

The 'Mets' ready to board the special trains at Paddington for South Wales. They were chosen because of their ease of mobilization and their experience in dealing with crowd disturbances

The 'Mets' are Sworn In at Tonypandy

The first contingent of Metropolitan police arrived in Tonypandy while some looting was still in progress.

A press account carried the story of their dramatic entry into the 'battered' town.

> '150 burly men, with unconcerned faces, tramping through the scene of the riot as calmly and firmly as though they were parading through Piccadilly Square.
>
> They marched through the town and back again during which they looked neither right nor to the left, and seemed oblivious of such stones as were flung at them, they then turned into the Skating Rink, not to be seen for nearly an hour, during which time the looters returned to the spoil.'

Apparently the march through Tonypandy was a piece of successful bluff as the 'Mets' had no legal rights to act as policemen until sworn in by local magistrates. It would have been illegal to charge except in self defence. They were marched into the local Skating Rink to await the magistrates and then returned to rapidly clear the streets without recourse to the use of batons. Walking in groups of 40-50, a firm "Get off home" succeeded in clearing the area.

The most eventful day in Tonypandy's history was over and peace had been restored at least for a time.

The mounted police ready for transportation to South Wales

The Role of Winston Churchill **The Arrival of The 'Mets'**

Metropolitan Police 'P' Division outside their Skating Rink billet, in the background their humorous placard ' Driven from home'

Mobilizing the 'Mets' many of whom lived in police barracks in London was relatively easy. Special trains sped them to South Wales

The Home Secretary, Winston Churchill, sent nearly 1,000 Metropolitan Policemen to the Valleys.

The Role of Winston Churchill **A Police State!**

Police Groups guard the Cambrian collieries

Merthyr Borough police one of the first contingents to be sent to the Rhondda at the request of the Chief Constable of Glamorganshire

The Role of Winston Churchill **Police Take Control of The Collieries**

All quiet at the Glamorgan Colliery, Llwynypia, with police tents erected in the grounds

The Role of Winston Churchill The Leaders: General Neville Macready

With the news of increasing violence and requests for the use of the military, Churchill, after consultation with officials of the War Office, decided to send General Macready to take command of the military in the valleys. Judging from his report to Parliament in March 1911 he was well suited for the task of protecting property without appearing to side with employers or workmen.

Macready set up his headquarters at 'The New Inn,' Pontypridd, which was an ideal location from which to direct operations in both the Rhondda and Aberdare Valleys.

Immediately he arranged daily meetings with the miners' leaders to act as a safety valve and turned down the coalowners requests for military to be used at the Combine Collieries.

He also gave express orders that his officers were not to accept any conspicuous form of entertainment from the coalowners. (The Chief Constable had no such reservation at accepting dinner invitations from Leonard Llewellyn.)

Although he described the mens' leaders as,

> *'indifferent workmen and generally without any stake in the locality",* he did add *"in justice to the strike committee in the Rhondda Valley, I must say that when they gave their word to me to carry out any undertaking it was scrupulously adhered to, a line of conduct which the employers might well have imitated.'*

His troops were never called upon to use their firearms but the presence of the military although in a mainly subordinate role to the considerable police force deployed in the valleys was effective in ensuring that the strikers failed in their main objective of preventing officials and blackleg labour from working.

Although the workmen were very critical of the behaviour of certain police contingents particularly the 'Bristols', the Cambrian Lodge Workmen's Committee stated that,

> *"Not one word against the military was ever uttered by the Combine Committee."*

Macready returned to London in January 1911, mission completed.

General Macready was very well thought of by Churchill as this letter suggests
"... expressing on behalf HM Government his (Churchill's) high appreciation of his services. He controlled a situation of great difficulty and has successfully avoided conflict between strikers and military. His impartiality between the interests of capital and labour will carry away respect and confidence of all different classes concerned in the dispute."
Home Office letter to War Office, 25 Dec 1910

The Role of Winston Churchill **The Leaders: The Men Who Ruled the Valleys**

Military and Police Chiefs controlling the Rhondda and Aberdare Valleys 1910-11
Front row left to right: Deputy Chief Constable; Sir. Neville Macready, the Chief Constable of Glamorgan, Captain Lionel Lindsay
Back row: Mr. Neame, Captain Harding, Chief Inspector Salter, Major Freeth and Captain Childs

D. Lleufer Thomas Stipendiary magistrate for the Pontypridd and Rhondda District.

He was a central figure in the use of troops but denied that the magistrates had requested them. He presided over the court cases against the miners.

J. F. Moylan was confidential adviser to Winston Churchill based in the Valleys. He sent regular reports to the Home Office about strike matters.

Sir Edward Troupe Under-Secretary of State at the Home Office

Sir E.R. Hendry – Metropolitan Commissioner of Police, New Scotland Yard

R.B.S. Haldane Secretary of State for war.

Keir Hardie M.P. and the Parliamentary Debate

In a debate at Westminster about the troubles in South Wales, Keir Hardie, the Member of Parliament for Merthyr and Aberdare, condemned the sending of the military. He voiced the view that was felt by many law abiding people in the affected area, that had there been half a dozen policemen on duty on the streets of Tonypandy the disorder would have been stopped (all policemen were concentrated at the Glamorgan Colliery half a mile from the town or were protecting coalowners' property). He felt that the presence of the soldiers 'was very offensive to the law abiding inhabitants.

> He stated that *'the number of men taking part in the window smashing never exceeded a 100.*
>
> *The military have been called out in connection with this dispute in South Wales, not only without any grave necessity, but without any necessity at all. There has not been any kind of disorder or disturbance with which the police force was not amply capable of dealing. If you take what is regarded as the very worst case of all, the Tonypandy window - smashing case, the number of men taking part in that window - smashing never exceeded 100, Local opinion is practically unanimous in saying that had there been 3 or 4 half a dozen policemen on duty on the streets when the window - smashing commenced, the whole of the disorder might have been stopped. But the whole of the police at this time with the exception of a few, were at the colliery guarding the owners' property.'*
>
> Extracts from Hansard, November 1910

Keir Hardie also protested at the unnecessary display of violence by the police. These matters were further discussed in Parliament later in November when he also enquired whether the troops had been sent at the request of the colliery owners.

Churchill listened to the complaints from the miners' M.P.'s but refused to hold an inquiry. This refusal earned him widespread condemnation in the South Wales mining valleys.

Rioting Renewed: 21st November 1910

In the days after the serious rioting of the 7th and 8th November the scale of protest was significantly lower with only sporadic incidents involving window breaking at officials houses. The authorities now had the military and over a thousand policemen under their charge to control the strike.

This relative calm was broken late in November when serious clashes again occurred between the police and strikers. On Monday 21st the miners resorted to vigorous picketing at Tonypandy and Llwynypia railway stations after rumours circulated that 'blacklegs' were being brought by train to the colliery premises.

A large crowd gathered at Tonypandy railway station but were refused permission to go on to the platform to search the incoming train. The refusal infuriated the crowd and some windows of the train were smashed. At the same time the sight of a drunken man being arrested by the police for smashing house windows at Trealaw further aroused an already hostile crowd.

At Llwynypia the signal box was targeted by between 400-500 strikers to get the signalman to stop all incoming trains to allow searches for 'blacklegs'.

At around 10pm at Penygraig an angry crowd used stones and bricks to hurl at the police who, in turn, made baton charges. Women joined the strikers and from bedroom windows showered boiling water onto the heads of the police in pursuit of the stone throwers.

Attacks and counter charges continued for some four hours with considerable injuries to both sides. Stretchers conveyed a few policemen back to their headquarters at the Skating Rink in Tonypandy.

As the situation appeared to be getting out of control police reinforcements were summoned. The cavalry from Pontypridd were quickly brought in and special trains brought police contingents from Pontypridd, Ystrad and other districts. The Lancashire Fusiliers stationed at Tonypandy were called out but took no part in quelling the disturbance.

This disturbance signalled the way that the Authorities would in future deal with confrontation calling in the military when the police were experiencing difficulty in establishing control.

During the disturbance, tradesmen hurriedly boarded their shop windows. In the early hours the roads were littered with stones, sticks and domestic utensils. Two arrests were made.

Riots Renewed in Mid-Rhondda.

Serious Street Fighting.

Strikers Hold Up Train.

Boiling Water Thrown Over Police.

The report by General Macready to the Home Office, 21 November 1910 shows how the authorities responded to the incidents

'It was reported during the day that four 'blacklegs" came up by the 1am train. They were spoken to by pickets on the station, and the porter who was on duty was informed that they had been taken to Trealaw and put in a shed until the next train to Cardiff. These are the men who were reported in the newspapers to have been thrown in the river. I can find no foundation for the statement.

….Mr.Llewellyn informed me he was getting in eleven men from Cardiff in order to keep the Glamorgan mine going at Llwynypia.

I heard for the first time that the strikers had interfered with a signalman on the railway, also a train at 1am on Sunday,36 hours ago

At 9.30 pm a report came via Pontypridd Railway station that the 8.30 train had been delayed by pickets for five minutes and that Tonypandy Station was besieged by large crowds of strikers and that the police were having a rough time, although they cleared the station.

At 9.50 pm Inspector Letheren, at Penygraig, reported the situation very serious and called for reinforcements.

….I immediately arranged, in the absence of the Chief Constable at Tonypandy, for the dispatch of 50 Metropolitan Police from the Pontypridd reserve by special train to Tonypandy Station, and at the same time telephoned to Major Freeth, who was stationed at Llwynypia to take a strong half company of the Lancashire Fusiliers and proceed at once to Penygraig…..a company of the West Riding regiment, was dispatched from Pontypridd to Tonypandy. A squadron of Hussars under Major Haag was sent at the same time to Penygraig by road.

The eleven men obtained by Mr. Llywellyn from Cardiff …were stopped at Pontypridd.'

Rioting Renewed: 1911: Events of the New Year

Western Mail cartoon depicting the miseries brought about by the strike

A rail crash in March 1911 at Hopkinstown, Pontypridd. Fourteen people were killed including three members of the Executive of the SWMF. As a result John Hopla and more radical miners were elected to the Executive

Headlines about the Trial of John Hopla: February 1911

A letter from the Chief Constable of Glamorgan to Sir E.R. Henry New Scotland Yard 16th, January 1911 prior to the trial of John Hopla. It shows the attitude of the police towards the miners' leaders and their desire to remove them from their positions of influence in the Rhondda.

Captain Lionel Lindsay describes in the letter the anxiety of the majority of the colliers whom he states wished to return to work.

"Irreconcilable minorities under the leadership of John Hopla and William John, the two most dangerous leaders at the present moment… are making a desperate effort to prevent them….I am pleased to report a good case of intimidation against John Hopla and William John, They will be tried as soon as possible. With these two men out of the way the movement must collapse."

John Hopla was on this occasion bound over for six months and fined £20 but later that year he was jailed with Will John for twelve months for 'unlawful assembly and rioting at Tonypandy on July 25th.'

Rioting Renewed: **Trial of Miners' Leader John Hopla: February 1911**

250 miners march through Tonypandy on 22 February 1911, in support of strike leader John Hopla. Hopla was summoned to appear at Pontypridd Magistrates Court on charges of intimidating three officials employed at the Glamorgan Colliery

Rioting Renewed: **(March 1911)**

Blaenclydach Shop Attacked
'A grocer's shop at Blaenclydach was the object of attack on Wednesday night. A crowd gathered, and a new road being in the course of construction at the spot, the mob were soon provided with ammunition, with which they pelted the premises.
Fortunately, P.S. Evans and a posse of police, who were parading the district, were soon on the spot, and charged the crowd with their batons. The Metropolitan Police, under the command of Inspector Hill, were soon on the scene, and succeeded in clearing the streets.'
Newspaper report.

Rioting Renewed: Penygraig and Clydach Vale (March 1911)

There was a renewal of violence in March 1911 linked to the intimidation of officials returning home from the Combine Collieries.

At 4pm on Thursday 23rd March, the police received information at their barracks at the Skating Rink Tonypandy that trouble was brewing at the entrance to the Ely Pit Penygraig. 60 Metropolitan policemen were hurriedly dispatched to the scene where they found a large crowd near the colliery entrance. A hostile reaction to the officials who were attempting to leave for home forced them to retreat back into the colliery yard. The arrival of the police led to the dispersal of the crowd which comprised of a considerable number of women.

Later that day at Blaenclydach there were more serious disturbances when colliery officials leaving the Cambrian Colliery were surrounded and threatened by a crowd of young men. A small body of police who rushed to the officials' assistance were met by a shower of stones, The police baton attacks not only failed to deter the strikers but in turn they were forced to retreat under a fusillade of stones. The confrontation drew an even larger hostile crowd who stoned the police from all directions causing injury and forcing two policemen to seek refuge in the nearby Central Hotel. The young strikers followed and the hotel windows were stoned. At this time the rioters were in full control. Police reinforcements hurried to the area, with 50 marching down from Clydach Vale and another 50 arriving from Tonypandy. Even with the additional 100 men the police had considerable difficulty in clearing the streets to get to the Central Hotel where most of the rioting was occurring.

The commotion led to large crowds gathering at street corners and stones being continually hurled at the police. Baton charges were made against around 200 strikers but the police were often driver back with both sides incurring injuries. The newly made roads provided an ample supply of ammunition. Later the strikers retreated to the mountainside where they continued stone throwing until they were eventually dispersed. The police had to patrol the area throughout that night.

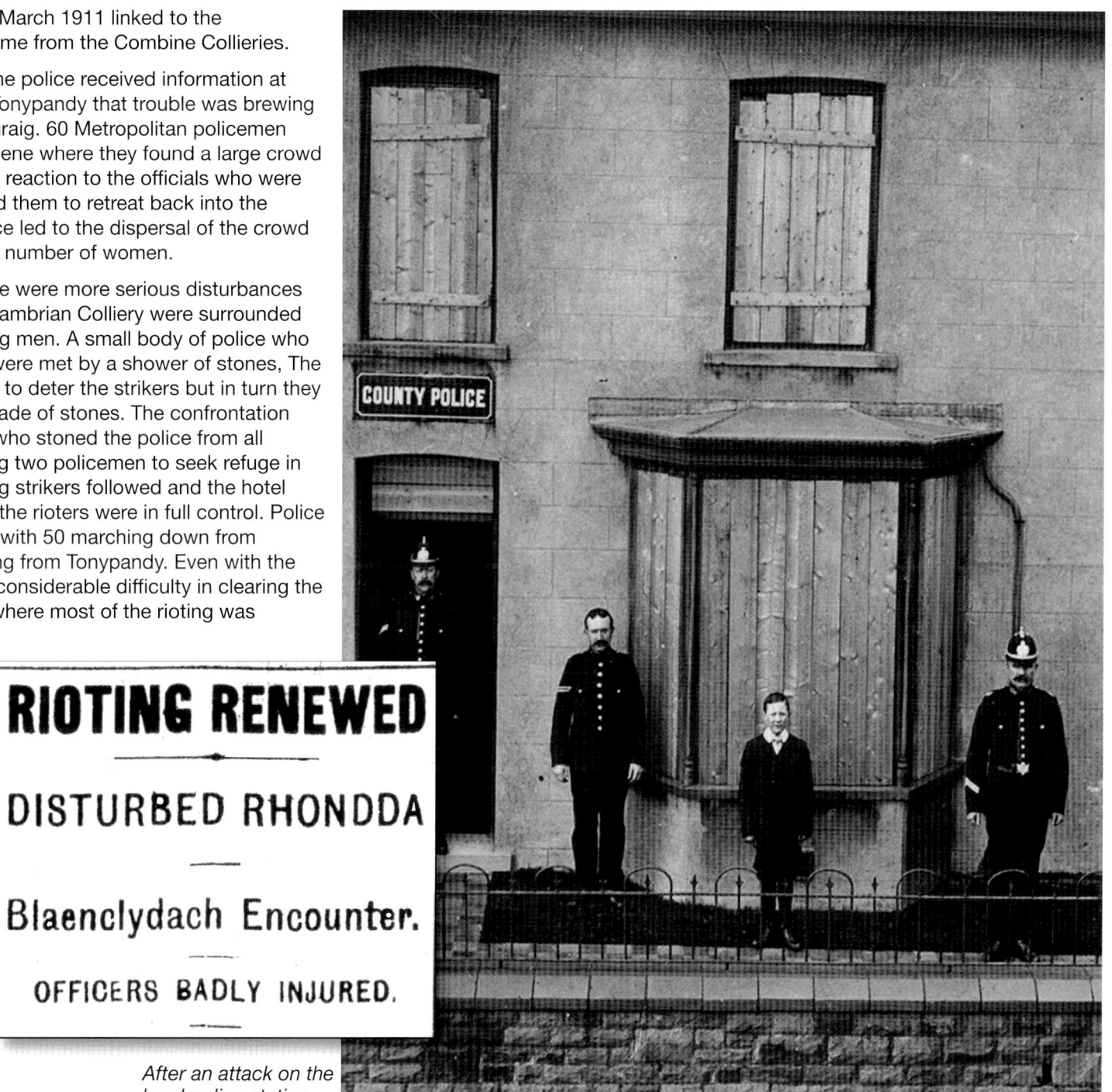

RIOTING RENEWED

DISTURBED RHONDDA

Blaenclydach Encounter.

OFFICERS BADLY INJURED.

After an attack on the local police station

Rioting Renewed: Attacks on Jones the Butcher, Clydach Vale (March 1911)

Police offer a reward to try to find the culprits who had burnt the slaughterhouse. It was never claimed

In March 1911, the property of a local butcher located at Clydach Vale a mile from the town of Tonypandy, was attacked. His shop windows were smashed and the following day, his slaughterhouse was burnt and his horse trap was wrecked.

Press reports suggested that the attack on the butcher's property was based on a rumour that a member of the Jones family had acted as a guide to the special police contingents which had been drafted into the area to deal with the new disturbances. The police denied the accusation, pointing out that with local officers who knew the area, they didn't need a civilian guide. Richard Jones the butcher's son offered £100 to be given to a charity if anyone could prove that he had guided the police as stated. There is no evidence that the money was claimed.

A second reason given for the attack was the financial benefit the family gained from part ownership of the Skating Rink at Tonypandy which had been taken over to accommodate Metropolitan policemen.

Rioting Renewed: Attack on Jones Butcher's Slaughterhouse (March 1911)

Miners and their families watch the slaughterhouse burning

EYE WITNESS: Gwen Cunningham witnessed the attack on the Slaughterhouse at Clydach Vale in 1911

"Up in Clydach near Blaen School. On the opposite corner was Jones the Butchers (on the side of the house was a picture of a cow). He was an old devil to people who owed him money - that's natural enough we know. They burned his books so that no one had to pay debt. They weren't satisfied with this so they took his trap up the mountain and let it down and smashed it to bits and then they burned his slaughter house down. That's the revenge they had. I saw the trap coming down, it came down almost even with St. Thomas. He had a wall dividing his land from someone else's, and so the miners took all the stones away. He used to move his wall near the other man's until he nearly had all the land. He wasn't very well liked."

A large crowd gathered on the hillside above Jones' slaughterhouse which had been set alight. No attempt was made to put out the fire. The Tonypandy Fire Brigade was unable to get to the building through the dense crowd and by 3pm the building was completely gutted and eventually looted.

Later the strikers took the butcher's trap further up the hillside, eventually releasing it and sending it hurtling down the mountainside to smash against a fence where younger members of the crowd finished its destruction.

What About The Horses?

During the second week of the official strike (November 7th, 1910), much publicity, both locally and nationally was given to the plight of some 300 pit ponies, still remaining underground at the Glamorgan Colliery, Llwynypia. Press reports inflamed public opinion with stories about ponies trapped underground without food and water and facing certain death from rapidly rising water. It appeared that the personal secretary to Leonard Llewellyn (a former press man) had given the story to a sympathetic pressman with the aim of discrediting the miners' leaders. This emotive issue was developing as an effective propaganda weapon for the coalowner. The miners as a consequence were subject to heavy criticism for what appeared to be their total disregard for the welfare of the animals. This resulted in the loss of a great deal of public sympathy for the miners cause.

There was no doubt that heavy picketing of the Glamorgan Colliery was having the effect of severely reducing the operation of the Powerhouse and the electricity generated to ensure that the huge pumps kept the underground workings free of water.

This editorial in the 'Morning Post' was typical of the stance taken by the press towards the miners' leaders,

> *'Perhaps no action of the strikers will arouse greater indignation than their attempt to condemn the pit-horses to death underground... By attacking the ventilating and the pumping machinery of the pits the striking miners sought not only the destruction of property but the lives of the unfortunate pit-horses below.'* (Morning Post, November, 11th 1910)

Further headlines referred to the interest shown by King George V in the plight of the ponies. This embittered the miners who were critical of the hypocrisy shown in concern for the welfare of animals but little for their wives and children. Confidential documents present a more balanced picture of the monarch's position, as King George had agreed to contribute to a Distress fund supporting miners' children but in the interests of impartiality his donation was to remain anonymous. Keir Hardie MP in supporting the miners stated in a Parliamentary debate on 19th November, 1910 quoting a mine manager,

> *'A dead pit pony is £20 loss: A dead collier costs nothing except heart-ache to those left behind'*

The miners response was to remind people that the situation had been deliberately engineered by Leonard Llewellyn who they felt had had ample time prior to the strike to bring out all the horses.

The fact that he also stabled pit ponies from neighbouring pits underground at his fortress, at the Glamorgan Colliery, aroused the suspicions of the miners leaders. They viewed his action as a ploy to try to deter them from using their main strike weapon of closing down the Powerhouse which in turn would prevent any work underground and inflict possible damage to coal producing seams.

The Press continued to be absorbed with the story. Later they reported that Leonard Llewellyn and two of his officials, had managed to descend the mine to find the horses in reasonable condition and were able to feed and water them. For this action Leonard Llewellyn and his officials were acclaimed national heroes for 'saving the horses'. He and his officials received several medals for this bravery including the Silver Medal of the Royal Humane Society.

Evidence suggests that the men's leaders were equally concerned about the condition of the horses but their offers of help were rejected by Leonard Llewellyn.

The men's leaders telegraphed Winston Churchill asking him to take immediate action on 'a matter of life and death'. Moylan, Churchill's personal representative at Tonypandy kept him informed of the situation. In his report of 12th November, he told Churchill that the miners' leaders were still prepared to supply sufficient men to bring up the horses and that the men were trustworthy. His report on 16th November made reference to the great resentment felt by the miners about the horses issue, and continued,

> *'it is quite clear that Mr. Llewellyn has been playing the horses off against the men. Mr. Llewellyn's stories of swimming in the mine to rescue the horses is hardly credible.'*

Later in the month of November all the horses were brought to the surface safely. This whole episode further embittered the men towards Llewellyn and his top officials.

The awards made to Leonard Llewellyn and his officials became the subject of constant jibes throughout the strike. A picture of a black cat on banners carried by the miners was intended to ridicule the awards made to Llewellyn. 'All he saved was a cat'.

In December 1910 a group of Gilfach Goch miners marched over the mountain carrying an effigy on horseback which caused great fun. It was meant to represent Leonard Llewellyn and was decorated with tin medals and a card on which was printed "For saving the horses".

WHAT ABOUT the HORSES?

What about the horses? The Evidence

THE POOR HORSES
"There are" said Mr. Llewellyn, about 900 horses in all the collieries of the Combine, and they have had no grub or water and very little air since last Sunday night. Besides, with a falling barometer there would be a lot of gas in the stables. There is a certain amount of moisture going down the pits."
Llewellyn's comments to a newspaper reporter November 1910

NAVAL COMMITTEE, CAMBRIAN COMBINE to HOME SECRETARY.

(Telegram: received at 6.45 p.m. on November 11.)

[Answered by No. 37.]

Will you immediately take steps in a matter of life and death. We the local officials have offered our services in assisting the management at the Cambrian Combine Collieries to raise and feed the horses. This has been refused. Blacklegs are introduced. If indeed you will assist us in putting down riots, send at once and stop this blacklegging. Otherwise as the local leaders we refuse to be held responsible for what is most certain to happen.—NAVAL COMMITTEE, CAMBRIAN COMBINE, PENYGRAIG.

The strikers leaders appealed to the Home Secretary to intervene to save the horses

---

The Horses are 'saved'
MESSAGE FROM LEONARD LLEWELLYN to MR R.G. ASKWITH at the BOARD OF TRADE
"Glad to say horses as far as we have been able to inspect them are all right and are now being fed and watered. Do not propose bringing them out of the mine this cold weather. No renewal of riots since the arrival of military. We shall now be able to look after horses without any assistance from outside."

ANXIETY OF THE KING.

MESSAGE TO THE RHONDDA.

"ARE THE HORSES STILL ALIVE?"

ANOTHER DAY FREE FROM STRIFE.

STOKERS TO BE IMPORTED.

We understand that King George, acting through the Home Secretary, has sent a message by wire to Major Fitzwilliam, who is in command of the cavalry at Pontypridd, and is now staying at the New Inn, inquiring most anxiously as to whether the horses in the mines of the Cambrian Combine are still alive.

Western Mail reports the King's concern

Food being brought for the horses

What about the horses? Medals for Leonard Llewellyn

Leonard Llewellyn was honoured by several national organisations for 'saving the horses'.

The Polo and Riding Pony Society presented him and one of his officials with medals and described them as ' The Welsh Mine Heroes', The presentation took place in March 1911 at the Hotel Metropole, London, and was made by Lord Arthur Cecil for the Polo and Riding Pony Society. Lord Cecil, in presenting the medals to both Leonard Llewellyn and to Mr. Hedley Clark an official, said,

> "their noble act was one of the most heroic ever performed in connection with the saving of animal life".

Mr. Llewellyn, replying, said,

> "As a Welshman he very much regretted that such a thing should have happened in Wales. The men no doubt lost control of themselves", He felt sure they were glad the ponies had been saved. He denied that pit ponies were ill treated; on the other hand, he asserted that many pit boys shared their dinner with the ponies."

Moylan's report to the Home Office 26/27th November 1910 provides a more objective assessment of what the situation was like.

In his report he criticised Leonard Llewellyn's comments in the press
> "On Saturday I descended number two pit at Glamorgan colliery, Llwynypia. Saw some of the rescued horses,..tended by an ostler and twelve officials.
>   The horses were without food and water from Monday morning 7th November to Thursday the 10th November and that they were all fed and watered on that date. Although admitting to difficulties they (the Combine's officials) agreed at once that the stories of swimming to save the horses were newspaper romances. The most they had to do was lead the horses through three feet of water. So far as I could judge the horses are in good condition."

RSPCA presentation made by the Countess of Bective to Leonard Llewellyn and his officials for 'saving the horses'

What about the horses? Medals for Officials

Mr. Evan Williams, Under-Manager of the Cambrian Colliery and the citation from a commemoration tray presented to him for the 'gallant rescue of a number of pit ponies'

Newspaper illustration of Combine officials 'saving the horses'

Evan Williams, Under-Manager of the Naval Colliery was awarded a medal for saving fifteen horses by the Dumb League of Friends and given a silver tea service by public subscription.

During the early part of the strike the family home was threatened by the strikers forcing them to move out of the area for their safety. After the strike he permanently moved his family to Afon Argoed to avoid any bitterness which lingered on about his role during the strike.

The whole episode aroused much anger amongst the miners and was not forgotten throughout the strike. It manifested itself in the ridicule aimed at Leonard Llewellyn and his medals.

Miners acknowledged that all Llewellyn had done was to save a black cat. Such was the acceptance in the community of this interpretation that at a meeting in the Theatre Royal late in November the appearance of a black cat placed on a table on the stage was greeted with much amusement

> *"Never was a turn witnessed which brought down the house so effectively as these purrings"* The Rhondda Leader

The black cat became an emblem portrayed on banners carried by the miners during their marches to Pontypridd in December 1910 in support of the Glifach miners summoned to appear there.

Mr. Llewellyn Williams and his Medal
"Great is the power of bunkum. Mr. Llewellyn Williams, the manager of the Cambrian Collieries is a very astute person. When his men worked their month's notice and came on strike, Mr. Williams decided not to bring the pit ponies to the surface. He knew that so long as they were underground there would be an excuse for keeping the colliery open and perhaps of his being able to smuggle down blacklegs. When the enginemen were induced to strike, Mr. Williams told a sympathetic pressman about the danger in which the poor ponies were thereby placed. They would get neither food nor water, nor air, and would probably all be dead, and for days the press rang with indignation at the heartless conduct of the striking colliers in inflicting wanton cruelty on the poor unoffending pit ponies. Even Mr. Stephen Coleridge and Mr. Cunningham Graham, in their indignation begotten of well-meaning but ignorant zeal joined in the hue and cry. After a day or two Mr. Williams descended the pit, found the ponies hale and hearty gave them a drink and a bunch of hay a piece and returned to the surface a national hero. How Mr. Williams must be smiling in his sleeve. But he must feel just a bit wee mean every time he looks at that silver medal and remembers how he came by it."
Labour Leader, November 18th, 1910

The critical editorial from the 'Labour Leader' publication about honours bestowed on a colliery manager for 'saving the horses' reflected the workmen's feelings.

Cambrian Horses Safe.
Officials Descend the Mine.

During Wednesday afternoon, the Cambrian officials descended the No. 2 Pit, Clydach Vale, in which there are 116 horses, and later in the evening they descended the No. 1 Pit, and went through the stables, and in each case the horses were found in good condition, and they were afterwards fed and watered. It was evident that the strikers were not aware that this course was to be taken. There was no demonstration at the pit entrance, and the officials were not interfered with in any way by the men.

At the Naval Collieries, where there are between 30 and 40 horses, the officials were unable to descend the mine, as the fires had been taken from underneath the boilers, but it is expected that the fires will be rekindled to-day, and that similar steps will be taken by the officials to feed the horses there.

Horses brought up from the Cambrian Colliery, Clydach Vale

Trial of the Gilfach Miners

Few prosecutions had been made in connection with the violence and looting which had occurred at Tonypandy in November. But early on Wednesday 14th December, bugle calls, a familiar sound to rally the men and their families, were heard throughout the strike communities. Miners from Gilfach Goch marched to Penygraig where in a remarkable show of solidarity, they were joined by thousands of other Combine strikers.

A crowd of nearly 10,000 men then marched down the valley on the six mile route to Pontypridd. Their show of support was for 13 of their fellow workmen from Gilfach Goch who had been summoned on charges under the Conspiracy and Property Act and of intimidating a colliery official. Music provided by the Hibernian and Llwynypia Drum and Fife Bands accompanied the men who sang to keep up their spirits. Women lined the streets at every vantage point to encourage the men. Shouts of 'Are we downhearted?' were quickly answered by the women *"No, No, No."*

At the head of the procession, which was a mile long, two standard bearers held aloft a banner bearing the grimly humorous legend "HUNGRY AS L- ions". The defendants all from the same mining village of Gilfach Goch wore their summonses defiantly pinned in their hats.

The Chief Constable of Glamorganshire, Lionel Lindsay and the Military under General Macready had made elaborate plans to defend the town of Pontypridd in case of an eruption of violence and looting which had occurred in Tonypandy on the 8th November.

Police and troops heavily guarded the Courthouse to which only the 13 accused were admitted. The miners continued their march around the town and climbed to the Common where they held a meeting around the historic Rocking Stone, overlooking the town.

The leaders are reported to have appealed for calm, pointing out that any attempt to march to the courthouse would be suicidal. Some of the younger element advocated taking violent action to free their colleagues should prison sentences be imposed. The trial lasted six days and each day thousands of miners marched from Tonypandy to Pontypridd but on the final day of the trial when sentences were to be imposed only a much smaller group of men appeared in Pontypridd.

The police and military presence on the final day was very strong with 400 police of whom a considerable number were mounted. They were supported by infantry from the Devonshire and West Riding regiments together with a squad of the 18th Hussars. They were deployed to block all entrances into the town.

Two of the strikers were given jail sentences. In anticipation of such convictions the authorities had made elaborate plans to transfer any convicted men quickly from the Courthouse to the prison at Cardiff.

The Military in readiness at Gelliwastad Road, Pontypridd

TRIAL of the GILFACH MINERS

Trial of the Gilfach Miners **The March to Pontypridd**

On Wednesday 14th December, 1910, an estimated 10,000 miners marched to Pontypridd In support of thirteen Gilfach strikers summoned under the Conspiracy and Property Act

Trial of the Gilfach Miners The March to Pontypridd

The strikers sang as they walked accompanied by the Llwynypia Drum and Fife band. They carried an effigy of a horse in mockery of the honours conferred on Leonard Llewellyn and his officials for 'saving the horses'

The orderly mile long procession passes the Merlin Bridge, Pontypridd. Notice the banner with the grimly humorous legend " Hungry as L..ions"

Strikers in Court.

Britannic Workmen Summoned for Assault.

Procession of Workmen March to Pontypridd.

Shortly after 5 o'clock on Wednesday morning the shrill note of a bugle blast resounded through Mid-Rhondda and Gilfach Goch calling the strikers together to march in a procession to Pontypridd Police Court, where a number of workmen were charged with using violence towards William Gould, assistant manager at the Britannic Colliery, Gilfach Goch, on 29th November.

Prevented by police and military from entering the town the men held a meeting at the Rocking Stone on the Common, Pontypridd

Trial of the Gilfach Miners Police and Military Cordon off The Town

Metropolitan police march through Pwllgwaun

Devonshire regiment guard Graigwen hill

A detachment of 100 Cardiff police were brought in for the occasion to add to the considerable number of mounted police and foot constables already in the area. (400 police in all). The army provided two troops of infantry, the Devonshire and West Riding regiments and a squadron of the 18th. Hussars.

PREPARATIONS FOR THE SENTENCE OF THE GILFACH MINERS

Sentences on the Gilfach strikers were delivered on Tuesday 20th December, 1910. Rumours circulated that if the Gilfach men were sentenced to imprisonment the strikers would attack the courthouse and rescue the men. The threats were taken seriously, resulting in the police and the military making elaborate plans for the 'defence' of the Courthouse and the town. The news of these preparations was deliberately conveyed to Tonypandy early that morning,

Pontypridd presented the appearance of a town under martial law.

The procession of miners was significantly smaller than on previous days. It was estimated that only 600 men had marched down the valley that morning as many had used their discretion and stayed away in case there was violence. Memories of the confrontation outside the Powerhouse, at the Glamorgan Colliery, back in November, the appeals for calm by the leadership and the very heavy presence of the police and military acted as restraining influences.

Pontypridd traders were advised to protect shop windows and not to leave goods on the pavements outside their premises. The whole community was in a state of nervous apprehension.

Trial of the Gilfach Miners **Market Square Pontypridd**

The West Riding Regiment in readiness for trouble at Market Square, Pontypridd

Trial of the Gilfach Miners **Taff Street Pontypridd (December 1910)**

Glamorgan, Metropolitan and Cardiff police guarding the town at Taff Street, Pontypridd, 20th December, 1910

Trial of the Gilfach Miners **The Final Day**

Arrangements to defend Pontypridd during the trial of the Gilfach miners sent by General Macready to the Home Office, 20th December, 1910

Location	Arrangements
Bridge off Porth Rd into upper part of town	To be blocked by police and a section of military
Exits from Town Mill St /Taff St	To be blocked by Metropolitan police backed by infantry /cavalry
Taff Vale railway station	Guarded by police and infantry
Exits from town towards Aberaman and Treforest	Cavalry patrols to keep watch
The following to be brought in	

Numbers	Unit
1 company	Loyal North Lancs.
1/2 company	West Ridings (from Rhondda)
1 Troop	18th Hussars (from Aberaman)
100 police	From Cardiff
100 Metropolitan police	From Rhondda
10 mounted	From Aberaman

Trial of the Gilfach Miners **Verdicts Delivered**

During the proceedings on the final day of the trial the police and military blocked access to the Courthouse in Gelliwastad road to all but those involved in the trial. Later in the day they allowed the few hundred strikers who had marched to Pontypridd in support of the accused to assemble outside the Courthouse to hear the verdicts. This was only done after the defendants found guilty, earlier, had already been transported by a special train to serve their sentences at Cardiff jail.

A report by General Macready to the Home Office December 1910

'All reports received since the trial began, confirm the impression that the bulk of the respectable strikers only take part in the procession not to lose caste with the more violent section (of the strikers) They are not in favour of the proceedings and have no wish to commit any act of violence. A strong minority see it as an excuse to create disturbance, not out of sympathy with the men being tried but to give vent to socialist ideas, continually preached in this valley.'

Trial of the Gilfach Miners **Verdicts Delivered**

Lleufer Thomas, the Stipendiary Magistrate for the district, delivered sentence.

Two of the strikers were jailed for 6 weeks, some were fined, one bound over to keep the peace, while charges against the remainder were dismissed.

The police and military then put into action a pre-arranged plan. The two strikers sentenced to imprisonment were smuggled out of the back door of the court and taken through the grounds of the property next door, St. Catherine's Church, to a char-à-banc which had been effectively screened by the troops on duty.

The vehicle took the prisoners and escorts to a special train which was waiting at a nearby railway goods yard belonging to the Taff Vale Railway Company. The specially commissioned engine and coach were ready to convey the men to jail at Cardiff.

The Court's decision was relayed to the miner's leaders only after the train was already heading for Cardiff. With little to be gained by remaining in Pontypridd, the marchers headed for home. By 2pm the town had returned to its normal appearance.

The heavy presence of the military to support the police had ensured that any attempt by the miners to storm the courthouse to try to rescue the Gilfach miners would have been futile.

Miners turn away from the Pontypridd Courthouse having heard the decision that 2 of the Gilfach miners had been sentenced to jail and were already being transported by train to Cardiff

Life During the Strike

The strike was to last for 10 months but for the Ely pit miners at the centre of the original 'Lock-out' there was to be no work for over a year. Without wages from 1st November, 1910, the miners and their families received small amounts of strike pay from the South Wales Miners Federation (SWMF) supported by a grant of £3000 a week from the Miners' Federation of Great Britain. This payment was stopped in July 1911 after the recommendation of the MFGB for a negotiated settlement was rejected by the Rhondda strikers. Married couples received 10/- a week and an additional 1/- for each child. The Cambrian Miners' Lodge committee also distributed tickets valued at 10/- which could be exchanged for food.

Hardship was inevitable for strikers' families but for non-unionist miners the plight was worse, for they did not receive any strike pay.

Additional funds came from public appeals. In the local area, Distress Committees were formed including representatives of the Board of Guardians, Workmen's Committees, school teachers and members of the Chamber of Trade. The records of canvassers from the distress committees provide graphic illustrations of conditions experienced by some families. In a house at Penygraig the visitor reported that she had seen a child with a baby lying dead in the room. Another canvasser recorded a case of a mother having to sell her bedclothes to buy food for her children, whilst a further report spoke of children crying for bread.

Newspapers claimed that within weeks of strike children were going to school without breakfast. Such was the concern of the Rhondda Education Committee that they implemented the Necessitous Children's Feeding Act passed by the Liberal government in 1906 enabling them to provide strikers' children with a meal on the five school-days.

Soup kitchens played a vital part in feeding the children and were set up in local chapels and clubs. They provided jugs of soup and occasionally meals of fish and potatoes. The Penygraig Constitutional Club, the Penygraig Conservative Club and the 'White Hart' public house at Tonypandy gave free meals on a daily basis to a number of children.

'Wholesale fish and vegetable companies from outside the area donated provisions which were distributed by the local Distress Committee. Later in 1911 miners dug allotments on the hillside which provided fresh vegetables whilst others reared chickens, geese and ducks for eggs and poultry. Public appeals for money were launched and the money raised was distributed amongst the needy. These appeals met with varying degrees of success. Traders who were initially supportive were divided after the outbreak of looting at Tonypandy and refused to contribute. Other traders not only made donations, but gave food on credit, until the decline in trading forced a curtailment of this practice.

In the early days of the strike, a donation of £2/14/6d was received from the police at the Cambrian Collieries and later families received support in the form of army rations unofficially donated by the regiments encamped in the Mid-Rhondda area. The Welsh Rugby Union donated £20 to the Rhondda Children's Distress Fund.

In December 1910 the Monmouthshire Education Committee resolved that the head teacher of every school in the County be asked to make collections amongst their scholars for feeding the school children in the Rhondda Valley and Aberdare.

Local theatre and cinema owners responded by introducing a lottery on admission ticket numbers with packages of food as prizes. Admission prices were reduced during the duration of the strike *'to members of the Miners' Federation and their families and sweethearts, provided they showed their union card.'*

Families in urgent need of money frequented the pawnshops. There were two in Tonypandy – Cardash and Freedman's.

During the strike and particularly during the difficult winter. Coal was in short supply. Levels were opened on the mountainside and the coal sold cheaply to strikers' families.

Given the range of evidence from the Distress committees, the schools and the newspaper reports, the conclusions of the Medical Officer of Health in his 1911 Report are surprising. (Although the report states that these were merely the opinions of inspectors.)

> *'the standard of nutrition continues to be good and no falling off was observed as a result of the strike in the Mid-Rhondda area which continued through the greater part of the year. A sufficiency of food was provided for the children affected from private as well as from public sources, the local education authority having contributed to the extent permitted by the Education (provision of meals) Act 1906.'*

LIFE DURING the STRIKE

Life During the Strike: Feeding the Children

The plight of strikers' children soon became a concern in the district leading to initiatives by both official and charitable groups. The matter was discussed by the Rhondda Education Committee on Friday 18th, November 1910. It decided to enforce the provisions of the School Meals Act. 1906 to make expenditure out of the rates. A sum of £600 was authorised. Attendance officers were tasked to collect information on those children in need.

Soup kitchens were also established by voluntary groups in chapels and public houses.

School teachers feed 'the necessitous children' with savoury soup and bread

Hardship for miners' families

"A Committee of Local Ladies met at 4.30pm to consider arrangements with regard to the feeding of necessitous school children. It has been arranged to commence feeding of such children according to the provision of the Act as soon as possible."
Log book entry, Llwynypia School (22nd November 1910)

'Penygraig Distress Fund: There were reports that children were going to school without having any breakfast- their needs were attended to by the schoolmasters and schoolmistresses. A donation was to be made to the schools to be given for such cases. Clubs in the area promised financial help.'
The Rhondda Leader (November 1910)

"With the approach of Christmas (there is) dejection and despair in the Rhondda Valleys. The women and children suffer most. They remain at home in silence which hunger has brought almost to all. The grates are fireless and many larders empty."
The Weekly Budget, 11 December 1910

EYE WITNESS:
"There was many a family that were half starved, but for the soup kitchens. Mention any school and it had a soup kitchen."

Treats to School Children.

Mr. James Edwards, builder, Tonyrefail, has given a sheep to the Penygraig Committee for the school children's dinner at Penygraig next Sunday.

Over 800 children were regaled with pie and other delicacies at the Theatre Royal, Tonypandy, on Saturday, by Mr. and Mrs. Sam Duckworth. A bioscope entertainment added materially to their enjoyment.

Life During the Strike: Shortage of Fuel

Children play their part picking coal from waste heaps near their homes (March 1911)

HOMES FOODLESS and FIRELESS
Babies Bathed in Neighbours' Houses

"Hunger and all the accompanying miseries of an industrial struggle are being severely felt in Mid-Rhondda. Empty larders may be counted by the score, and although every effort is made to cope with the distress, many of the most deserving cases are reluctant to make their necessity known, preferring to suffer in silence.

The absence of coal adds very materially to their sufferings in the cold and bitter weather. All of the surrounding rubbish tips have been so thoroughly cleared of any scraps of coal that might be left about, that the strikers, armed with picks, hammers and other implements have been digging in the vicinity of tipping screens to relieve their distress. Mothers of young babies, some of the latter being babies a few weeks old, gather at the houses of their more fortunate neighbours where there still remains a little fire to bath their young, while other women still more unfortunately placed suffer pains of accouchement in desolate homes where the embers of the last fire have ceased to glow."

From a newspaper report, December 1910

EYE WITNESS: Sarah Ann Jones
"We lived on 11/- a week for man/wife and one child. (Pay was £3/12/- a fortnight) My husband was a haulier with the horses. There were soup kitchens for the children at Pontrhondda School. For adults there was the old baths at Llwynypia for meals. We didn't use them, we were very good sure. We never went without our Sunday dinner. I used to buy a ham bone 1/6 to last all the week. My husband had an allotment at the back of the house where we grew all our food - there were several allotments where the Llwynypia College of Further Education is now. For coal the men went to open levels on the mountainside."

During the hard winter of 1910 miners opened illegal coal levels on the mountain side to provide cheap coal, Three were fined by magistrates for taking coal in a case brought by the Naval Colliery Company. They were 'caught at a level, 'mandril' in hand and three hundred weights of coal valued at 3/-.

Life During the Strike **Receiving Strike Pay**

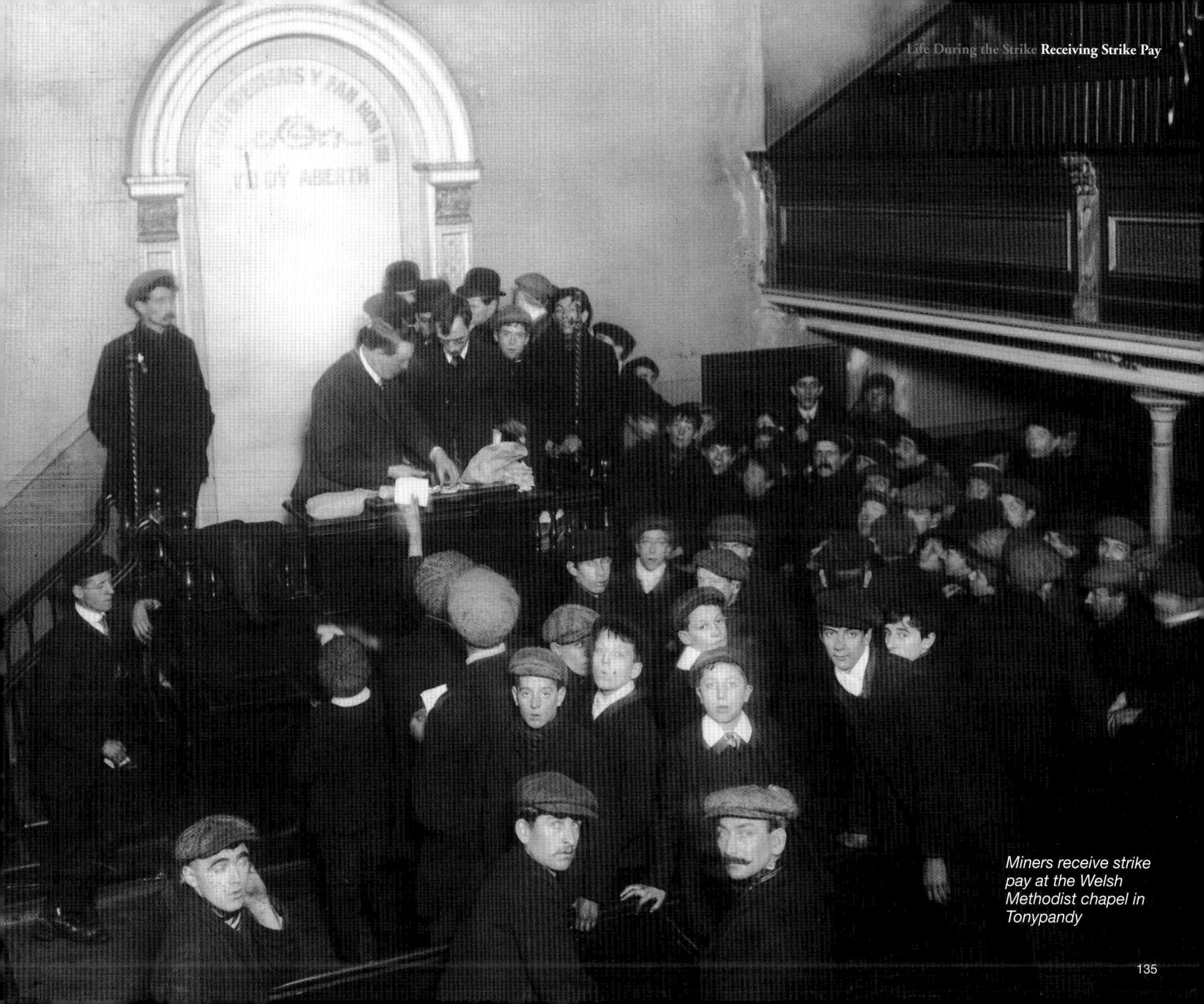

Miners receive strike pay at the Welsh Methodist chapel in Tonypandy

Life During the Strike: How We Lived

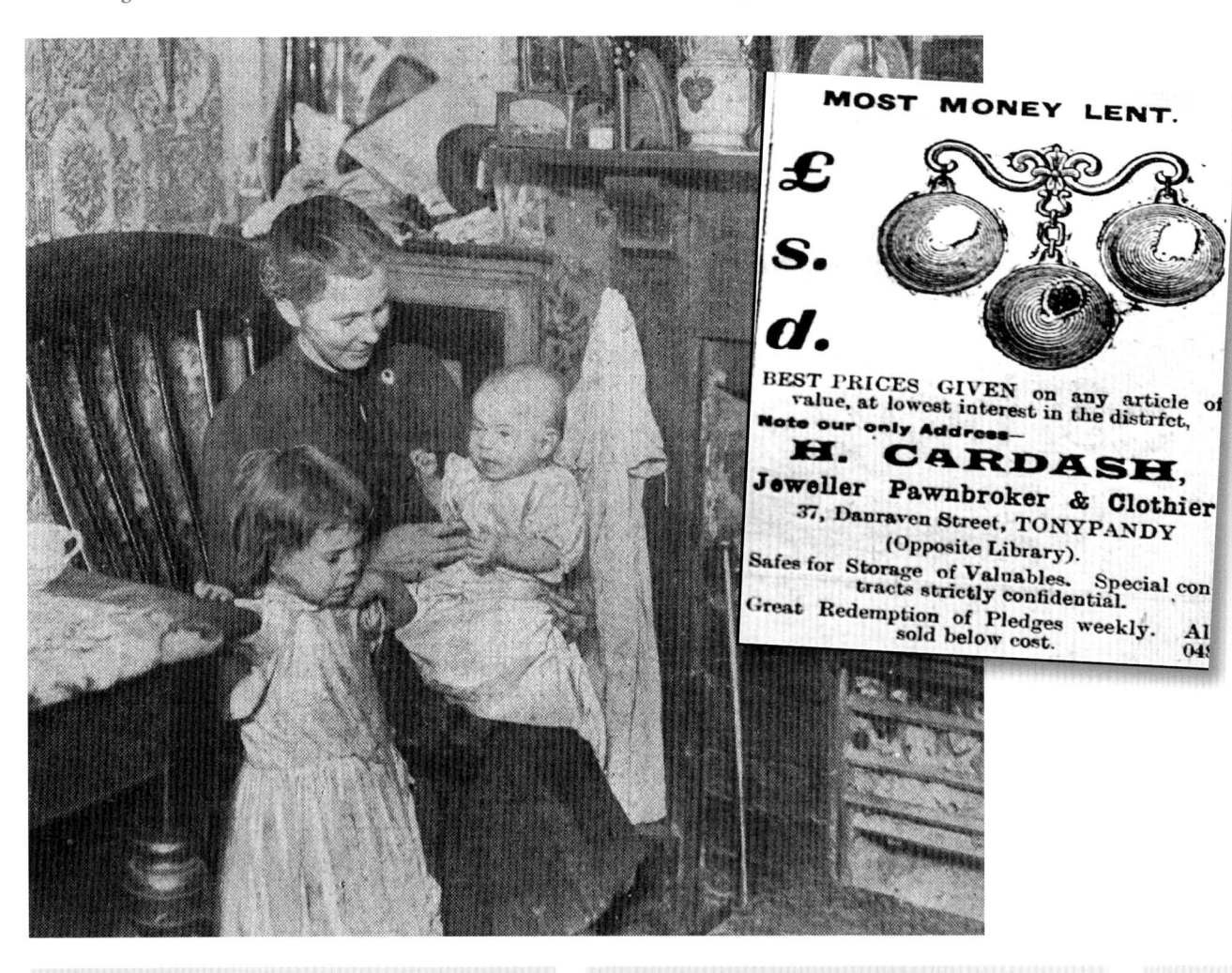

MOST MONEY LENT.

£ s. d.

BEST PRICES GIVEN on any article of value, at lowest interest in the district.
Note our only Address:—
H. CARDASH,
Jeweller Pawnbroker & Clothier
37, Danraven Street, TONYPANDY
(Opposite Library).
Safes for Storage of Valuables. Special contracts strictly confidential.
Great Redemption of Pledges weekly. All sold below cost.

WORKING MEN of the Rhondda Valley

Can do no better than call on the "Old Firm"

FREEDMAN & SONS,

The Mid-Rhondda Pawnbrokers,

TONYPANDY,

For real good value in every description of

Working Clothes.

Absolutely the largest and most varied Stock

of Second-hand Goods

in Wales to select from.

Before making your Winter Purchases it will well repay the Working Man of all classes of trade to GIVE US A CALL.

Our Special Feature :—**CHEAPNESS** consistent with the Best of Value for Money.

Business increased rapidly for the two pawnbrokers in Tonypandy

EYE WITNESS: A Clydach Vale Resident.
"There was hardship with only 10/- a week and 1/- per child coming in. We were lucky it was a mild winter and a beautiful summer. But soon clothes and shoes began to wear out - we were very fortunate that we had help from a family living in the same street as us. The husband was working in the Gorki Pit and so they had money coming in. For coal you went to the levels to stake your claim - no one would take your level but if someone didn't have coal for a fire in winter they were given some."

EYE WITNESS: The pawnshops
*"As the strike went on, and things became more difficult, people were forced to pawn goods. There were several pawn shops in the area for example Freedman, and Cardash.
If you wanted to pawn something you went down the gully to the side door so that you were not seen. Many people took their best clothes to the shop on a Monday morning, and went back to have them redeemed on Friday (pay day), so that they could have them for the week-end."*

EYE WITNESS:
*"My father was a coal miner. There was not much food because we didn't have the money to buy. But my father had an allotment in which he grew all kinds of vegetables and we had our own poultry for fresh eggs.
A lady in William Street died with many people owing her money. She gave away money rather than see people starve. There were also soup kitchens to feed the children and the wives. People dug into the coal tips to get their coal. Clothes were altered and handed down from one child to another. All the savings were used up."*

Life During the Strike **Business as Usual**

An enterprising baker offers his large 8 lb. loaves at reduced prices for as long as the strike lasts

CHAMBER'S MAGNANIMITY.

Despite the recent destruction to property during the riots, the Chamber members wished to show that there was no animosity amongst them, and the subject of the acute distress caused by the strike in Mid-Rhondda received great consideration.

Mr. Llewellyn Evans stated that the Chamber had collected and sent a special donation to the Distress Committee in the early stages of the struggle, and the Committee had highly appreciated the action. The distress must be tenfold more to-day, and there was dire need of funds. He believed that the best class of colliers thoroughly disagreed with the action of those who had caused the damage. The speaker proposed that circulars be sent to every tradesman in the locality calling his attention to the prevalent distress.

Mr. J. Rees seconded the proposition which was heartily supported by Mr. Owen Jones and others.

It was also decided to write to the various Chambers of Trade affiliated the Federated Chambers of Trade South Wales, asking them if they could assist in alleviating the suffering in Mid Rhondda.

THEATRE ROYAL, Tonypandy.
ELECTRIC BIOGRAPH NIGHTLY.

Monday, November 21st, and during the Week,
Mr. F. B. WOULFE & COMPANY
In a Repertoire of well-known Plays (for particulars see bills).

☞ ALL MEMBERS OF THE MINERS' FEDERATION
(Showing their Cards),
Also their WIFES, DAUGHTERS and SWEETHEARTS
will be admitted at **3d.; 6d.; 9d. and 1/-**
Usual Prices for those not showing Cards.

The Rhondda Leader Report, November 1910
'At Pisgah Vestry, a Distress Committee was formed, presided over by Mr. Joseph Jones, member of the Board of Guardians. £35 has been distributed by the lodge. Visits had been made to some houses and it was found that in some there wasn't anything to eat. The Committee was composed of the Workmen's Committee, schoolteachers and the Chamber of Trade.'

EYE WITNESSES: Harry Hobbs, a Cambrian miner
"The miners and their families could go to soup kitchens. Sometimes they used to have cod heads. These were hard times to see little children running around in knickers made from sacks."

W.J. Morris
"As the strike brought in no money some wives made trousers for their men out of sacks. After the sacks were worn they turned them inside out."

Life During the Strike: Catering for the Police

Catering staff supplying daily meals to hundreds of policemen patrolling the Valleys

During the second week of November the arrival of hundreds of Metropolitan police caused considerable accommodation and catering problems. The bulk of the 'Mets' were housed at a local Skating Rink a large draughty, inhospitable skeleton building. In the early days those not on duty had to lie on the floor in their duty clothes and with conditions so cold few could sleep. Men tramped up and down throughout the night to try to keep themselves warm. Breakfast consisted of bread, cheese and ginger beer with little to eat during the rest of the day. For a few days no officer was able to wash.

Hotels, public houses, large houses, drill halls and theatres were also used as lodgings.

EYE WITNESS: Lilly Pontsford
Her father continued to work at the Glamorgan Colliery as he was on compensation due to a shot firing accident.
"There was a lot of police living on the colliery after because I can remember my father used to bring their underwear home for my mother to wash."

'Free House', The Thirsty Nine' Christmas 1910, The 'Mets' enjoy their Christmas at the Drill Hall, Pontypridd

Life During the Strike **Accommodating the Police**

In December 1910 a heavy storm forced a contingent of Mets to be evacuated from the Skating Rink to Llwynypia school which closed to children for four days. The children continued to be fed in the infants department.

Skating Rink Partially Unroofed.

Metro's "Moved On."

The Tonypandy Rink suffered greatly from the terrific storm on Friday. The wind dislodged several sheets of corrugated iron and ripped about 12 yards square from each side of the roof. This made it impossible for the Metropolitan Police to stay there, and they had to shift their quarters to the Hippodrome for the night.

Several windows have also been smashed.

EYE WITNESS: Edith Hancock
'They (the police) slept in the Rink see, but whether it was true I don't know, but he used to tell my mother and me that...... 'Mind we didn't come up there', whether he'd done it to frighten us because they're 'sleeping with the rats'. The rats was crawling all around.'

The Skating Rink at Tonypandy was commandeered as accommodation for the Metropolitan police in November 1910 and remained a police base throughout the dispute.

Owned by J. Owen Jones and family it aroused strong feelings against them. They were seen to be benefiting from rents paid by the authorities.

Tea Break using improvised catering facilities

Life During the Strike **Accommodating the Police**

The obligatory photograph but with a touch of humour !

Life During the Strike **Accommodating the Police**

A much needed stove provides warmth in the winter 1910-11

The 'Mets' leaving the Skating Rink Tonypandy for London, March 1911

Billeting the large number of police and military was a major problem. Hotels, public houses, a skating rink and drill halls were used but in winter they were often very uncomfortable. At Christmas, the places were decorated and concerts held to provide a little light relief.

Life During the Strike **Accommodating the Police**

Eye Witness: Gwen Cunningham a maid to Leonard Llewellyn's family at Glyncornel House

"I worked for Mr. Leonard Llewellyn for twelve years at Glyncornel and during that time the strike occurred and the police took over the house. They were billeted there and we had to leave. Captain Lindsay took over the house and after he left the soldiers were billeted there. When we returned it was in a filthy condition, the tables were covered in grease."

Glyncornel House the home of the Combine's General Manager Leonard Llewellyn, which was requisitioned as a billet for the police during the strike

Life During the Strike **Fraternization**

Police pass the time teaching young boys the art of boxing

Life During the Strike Farewell to the Soldiers

The Soldiers Farewell Lancashires Leave Tonypandy - Scenes of Bustle and Excitement

The departure of the Lancashire Fusiliers and the arrival of the Somersets created a stir in Tonypandy on Friday last about 11.30. A special train arrived at Tonypandy (T.V.R.) bearing 300 soldiers of the Somerset regiment. Crowds had assembled along the highway to witness the "march past".

Early in the morning the offices where the Lancashires were stationed were scenes of general bustle and business. Large crowds had assembled around the offices, and watched the army men packing their kit ready for travelling. Many regret the departure of the Fusiliers as they had become very popular during their stay in the "strikers' quarters" especially in football circles, where they were most successful. At the time of the departure thousands were assembled along the streets, and while marching to the station (Tonypandy T.V.R.) a large number followed in the soldiers' wake. On Trealaw Bridge hundreds were waiting to see them off, many sitting on the coping of the walls to have a good view of the station. Points of vantage surrounding the station were all taken up. No persons were allowed on the platform without tickets, but in spite of this precaution, crowds gained entrance to the station to wish their soldier friends a final adieu. After boarding the train (a special G.W.R.) the Fusiliers crowded round the windows shaking hands with their many friends. On the departure of the train a rousing cheer was given to the soldiers, which was answered by the "defenders of Britain." Cheering continued until the train was out of sight.

The Rhondda Leader, March 1911

Whereas there was strong criticism of certain police contingents especially the 'Bristols' relationships with the military were invariably good.

At a Socialist Democratic Conference at Coventry during April 1911 a Mr. Wilkinson of Blaenclydach, Rhondda said, '...one credible fact was that the military to a man had taken the side of the men (cheers) and for that reason had been removed from the district. One body of military had been removed on account of their constant conflicts with the police' (laughter)

Western Mail, 17th April, 1911.

Life During the Strike: The Miners' Ballot March 1911 and Renewed Rioting

Discussion about ending the strike had intensified in the new year resulting from the strain on miners' families during the winter and the depletion of the MFGB funds. Pressure was building to arrive at a settlement and on Wednesday 22nd March 1911 delegates from the SWMF and representatives of the MFGB arrived in Tonypandy. They were there to convey to the strike committee a decision which had been taken the previous day at a Federation Council in Cardiff to call a ballot.

The Federation representatives during their walk to the meeting at Moriah Chapel, Tonypandy ran the gauntlet of strikers shouting 'No ballot!', 'We won't have a ballot boys!' At the meeting the delegations insistence on a ballot infuriated the more militant strikers and later the Federation representatives needed police protection on their return to the railway station. MFGB delegate W.E. Harvey MP commented to the press

> *"I was never treated so badly in all my life as I have been today ...I have never been treated so unfairly as I was at Tonypandy. They began before they knew what I had to say, or what our policy was. If disputes are conducted on such lines...the end is not far off for all Trade Union Movements."*

A mass meeting of over 5,000 men was called at the Mid-Rhondda Athletic Ground. William John, Chairman of the Joint Committee, addressed the gathering and strongly criticized the Executive Council for trying to enforce a ballot to return to work on the previously negotiated terms of October 1910. Resolutions were passed condemning the SWMF and a march was arranged to the Cambrian colliery at Clydach Vale, which was guarded by 54 constables, reinforced by a further 100 policemen along the railway line.

The strikers occupied the high ground above the colliery and some stoning of the police took place until the men were dispersed by police baton charges,

The following day more violence occurred at Clydach Vale outside the Bush Hotel against the police who were escorting nine officials from work. Windows were smashed and one shop looted. It was reported that the rioters were chiefly youths aged between 16 and 22.

A butcher's shop in Clydach Vale was attacked on Friday 24th March and a large crowd turned up to witness the burning of the butcher's slaughterhouse and surrounding out-buildings.

On the Saturday 25th March, a ballot about settling the strike was held in the Mid-Rhondda with a large majority of miners voting to continue the strike.

The press described the voting process as farcical when it was known how the voting slips were used. Each miner had been given 2 counterfoils stating 'For' or 'Against'. It was reported that the strike committee conducting the ballot had distributed pins to strikers and instructed them to "show their true colours" after they had voted by displaying in their cap lapels the part of the balloting slip which they had not cast. The press criticised what they termed a violation of the secret ballot and the intimidation of miners who had voted for a return to work. The voting was 7,041 against accepting the terms, with 309 for 5,000 men did not vote.

A Western Mail cartoon suggesting anarchy was again on the prowl in the Rhondda Valley

Major Freeth, who had replaced General Macready in charge of the military wrote in his report to the Home Office that the six officials conducting the polling booths were the most rabid socialists leaders in the district and that the ballot result was regarded as a foregone conclusion.

Life During the Strike **Life Goes On!**

In July 1911 the YMCA held its first Annual Garden Party at Gilmour's field overlooking the now silent strike torn Glamorgan Colliery, Llwynypia. The event was well attended with tea provided on the field, games played included a confetti battle between the YMCA and the Shop Assistant Ramblers. The event ended with a concert

Final Days Confrontation: Ely Pit 25th July 1911

The last major confrontation of the dispute occurred in July 1911 at the Ely Pit, Penygraig, the scene of the 'lock-out' which had precipitated the Cambrian Combine strike, Both William John and John Hopla the miners leaders were summoned as a result of the disturbance.

Rhondda Riots Renewed Fierce Attack on Ely Pit, 18 Police Hurt

Rumours were circulating in the district that men were returning to work. A mass meeting of workmen was held at Tonypandy on 25th July 1911 followed by a procession to the Ely pit by over 2000 miners. The marchers were loudly cheered by women folk as they passed near to the village of Penygraig.

The men took up positions on the hills above the pit, and violence erupted when the police were seen to be escorting a man known to be working at the Ely. Stones were hurled from the mountainside demolishing part of the roof of the colliery engine house. Women joined the men and collected loose stones in their aprons to provide relays of ammunition.

Police baton charges were ordered but failed to dislodge the men. It was not until the arrival of 80 soldiers from the Somerset Light Infantry, who took up positions on the mountain armed with fixed bayonets and ball shot in their guns, that the police eventually gained control. The tactic used by the soldiers was to drive the workmen down into the village where the police again charged and dispersed them. 18 policemen were injured mainly by stones. There were few casualties to the workmen who had kept their distance and had evaded the baton charges. The few strikers who were caught were severely dealt with.

The seriousness of this incident led to the further mobilization of the military and that evening they paraded the streets with the police. The following day saw an uneasy calm in the district and a further mass meeting was held. Two young officials of the Glamorgan Colliery were 'kidnapped' and frog-marched through the town of Tonypandy before the police intervened to rescue them. The increased gravity of the situation, resulted in extra police being drafted to the area supported by troops from the West Ridings with the Lancashire Fusiliers being quartered near to the Glamorgan Colliery.

Report from the Western Mail, 26th July 1911.

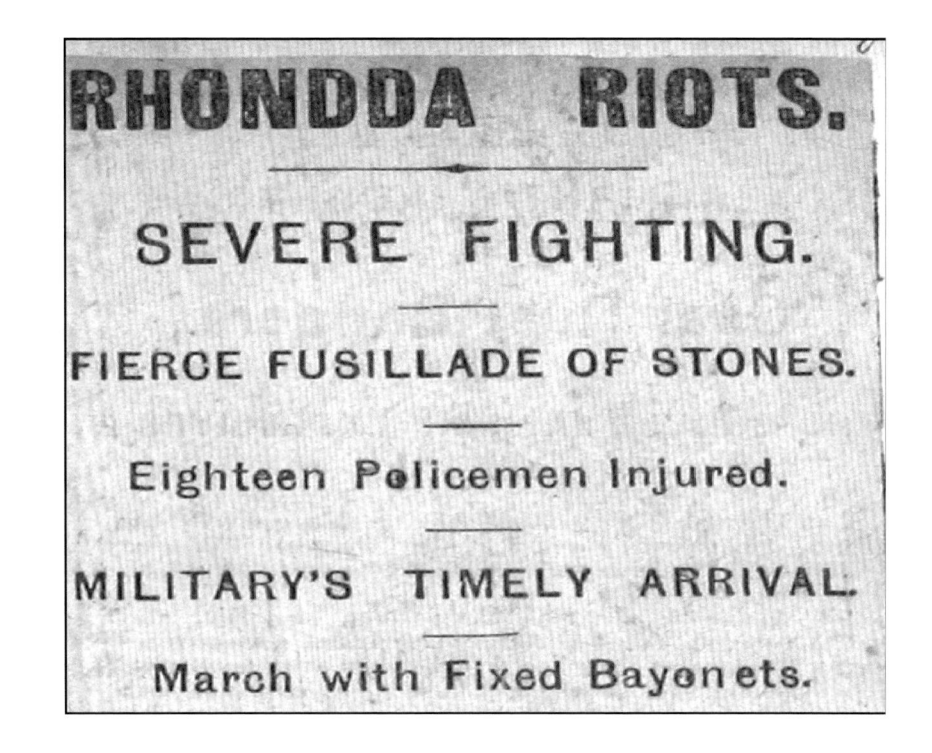

RHONDDA RIOTS.

SEVERE FIGHTING.

FIERCE FUSILLADE OF STONES.

Eighteen Policemen Injured.

MILITARY'S TIMELY ARRIVAL.

March with Fixed Bayonets.

The following letter written by a policeman involved in the Ely Pit disturbance of the 25th July was sent to a senior officer based at Pontypridd.

Sir,
I beg to report that about 2.45 p.m. on Tuesday 25th July 1911, being told to accompany A.S. 423 Thomas and other constables to mingle and prevent a crowd of strikers above the Ely Pit Engine House Penygraig to throw stones at the Engine House. One pane of glass had already been broken, when proceeding through the quarry in Hendre–Gwilym behind the Engine House a large number of stones were thrown at us the (Police) from the bank above. I was struck several times on the helmet, the last stone knocked it off my head down the bank, the stones were coming too thick to enable me to fetch it at the time, and we were obligated to retire. About a quarter of an hour afterwards Insp Williams instructed me and P.C. 36 Ashford to go and look for more helmets and also to bring P.C's 340 Ballard helmet back. When we get into the Quarry we were again pelted with stones and again obliged to retire. I informed Insp Williams and he told me that one of the men who threw stones at us was Jack Hopla's brother. They were all strangers to me.
I am sir,
Your obedient servant
John Jones P.C.141

Final Days The Achievement?

In August 1911 the tenth month of the strike and a year since the 'lock-out' of the Ely pit miners, newspaper headlines reflected a mood of optimism that at last the dispute was near to settlement. 'Hopes of peace in Mid- Rhondda'; 'Probable Settlement of Cambrian Dispute'; 'Men may resume work this month'.

Divisions had appeared between the local strike leaders and their national organisations. Some strikers felt that the campaign had gone as far as was possible. It was time to heed the advice of the MFGB to accept terms similar to those which William Abraham had negotiated prior to the strike but with the establishment of machinery to deal with disputes about seams.

When the Cambrian Workmen's Committee rejected the advice of the MFGB to settle, the national organisation decided to 'wash its hands' of the dispute and voted to stop providing the £3,000 weekly financial aid. Dwindling reserves and the prospect of another winter without work led the South Wales Miners' Federation also to recommend a return to work.

Even at this late stage the leaders of the Cambrian Combine workers Joint Committee were still campaigning for a national stoppage linked to the central issues of abnormal places and the minimum wage. On the 16th August a meeting at Tonypandy with members of the SWMF was adjourned for a day because of dissension and lengthy discussions. The next day the men voted for a return to work and passed the following resolution:

> "That the Combine workmen adopt the recommendations of the executive council to return to work, and also resolve that the foregoing be accepted under protest against those who have been guilty of such frigid indifference to the Cambrian workmen in this dispute."

Talks opened up with the individual coal companies and the respective lodges and work finally resumed on the first Monday in September 1911. It took several months before work was resumed in all collieries. The Naval pit could not start because of shortage of pitwood and delays in other pits resulted from innumerable falls which had to be cleared and air passages which had to be repaired and made safe. This was particularly evident in the Naval pits which had been shut for over a year. One of the most bitter conflicts in the story of industrial relations in the British coal industry was over.

What was achieved by the strike?

The men who returned to work in September 1911 might well have felt that their efforts had been in vain, for they had failed to win an improvement on the cutting price which William Abrahams 'Mabon' had negotiated in October 1910 just before the strike. The cutting price remained at 2/1¾d. per ton of coal as against the men's demands for 2/6d. a ton.

But there were recognisable achievements as the following historians have identified:

R. Page Arnot

> 'The Cambrian Combine miners had been made 'to eat the leek' but their tears had watered the growth of a much greater leek which in less than a twelve month the owners were forced to chew upon and then to swallow'

Although the miners lost the local dispute the crucial issue of "abnormal places" had become a national issue and later culminated in a demand for a National Minimum Wage which was achieved by Act of Parliament after the National Strike of 1912. The minimum wage meant that wages would no longer be dependent entirely on the amount of coal cut.

Historian Dai Smith concludes

> "It is not too much to claim that the Minimum Wage Act, one of the most important landmarks in the history of coal-mining unionism in this country, was essentially the outcome of an agitation that had its origins in the Rhondda Valley, that is, the Cambrian Strike."

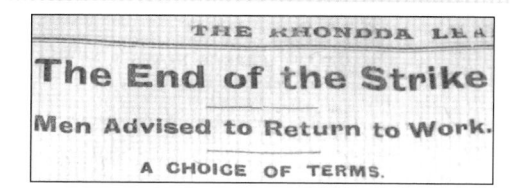

THE RHONDDA LEA
The End of the Strike
Men Advised to Return to Work.
A CHOICE OF TERMS.

Historian Louise Miskell

> "The dispute had some identifiable legacies, notably the publication the following year of The Miners' Next Step and the emergence in the leadership of the South Wales Miners' Federation of some of the prominent figures from the dispute..."

During the 10 month strike over 1 million in wages had been lost and there had been much hardship for miners' families and for those whose livelihood depended on miners' spending. For some families the suffering was to continue long after the strike was over, as the owners were initially unable to find work for over 3,000 men. It was estimated that losses amounted to over £3.5 million from wages, loss of profits, loss of trade, house rents and the cost of damage to property.

Families uprooted and left the district to find work and figures for local recruitment for the armed forces was the highest ever.

If the strike was settled the costs of keeping 'the armies of occupation' were not. The Glamorgan Coal Company resorted to litigation against Glamorgan County Council to recover the costs of catering, housing and supplying food for the hundreds of policemen drafted into the Rhondda. Finally in 1916, a settlement was made of £10,000 in favour of the Coal Company.

Memories of the bitterness seemed to have faded by January 1912 when D. A. Thomas received warm applause from workmen at the Cambrian Colliery, Clydach Vale during a ceremony to cut the sod of the new nos.4 pit which would lead to the creation of a further 1,000 jobs.

But some things were not to be forgotten and in a changed political context repeated battles were fought In the press and on election platforms about the role of one of the central figures in the dispute, Winston Churchill.

Captain Tupper addressing a meeting in Cardiff

Captain Tupper was known as a firebrand and has been described by Lord Birkenhead as the most dangerous man in Europe who wants to drench this country in blood from John O'Groats to Lands End.

> After Tupper's address to the Rhondda miners, a report was sent to the home office, 2nd August, 1911 which provides an interesting alternative view
>
> *'Captain Tupper pointed out that rioting was a relic of the dark ages. Expressed regret that they had ever taken place. He asked the men to refrain in future as it would prejudice their cause, His strong recommendation was to resume work. He staked his word that neither they or the owners could be said to have given in. He gave them his assurance that an outside pressure had come to bear on the situation the precise nature of which although known to him, he was not in a position to make known to them but it would bear on the owners as well as the men.'*
>
> A Home Office spokesman on the 3rd August described Tupper as 'an angel of peace'. The men agreed to end the strike at a meeting on August 17th, 1911.

> **Captain Tupper at Tonypandy**
> Characteristic Address to the Strikers
>
> *One of the largest meetings ever held on the Mid-Rhondda Athletic Grounds was addressed on Wednesday afternoon by Capt. Tupper, Mr. Chas Damn (secretary of the Cardiff branch of the Seamen and Firemen's Union) and Mr. W Trainer (ILP organiser Cardiff) Mr. W. John (Chairman of the Cambrian Workmen's Joint Committee) presided.*
>
> *Mr. Trainer was the first to speak, dealt with the seamen's strike at Cardiff and emphasized its outstanding lessons, viz., the solidarity of the workers, and the interdependence of one class of labour upon the other.*
>
> *Capt. Tupper had a magnificent reception on rising to speak. " It is a great honour and pleasure to me to come and address you for the second time," were his opening words. "I had only a short time with you last week, as we had to go back to Cardiff because they were going to start work, and I wanted to see that the men had their 'jimmy O'goblins' (laughter). We weren't taking any chances," he continued, "you can't trust the capitalist class too long."*
>
> *He then proceeded to detail the points won by the seamen at Cardiff, and said that the example set by the Bristol Channel men was the greatest example of solidarity the world had ever seen. The men had now a wage of £5 a month, and if the freights went up, the skipper (as he termed himself) would be on the spot again to see that the men had £5/10/- according to the agreement. They had won a sensational victory at Cardiff through solidarity of the workers, and he wanted the men of Mid-Rhondda to emulate that example The capitalists and monopolists could never withstand the workers when they were united. "Imagine", he said, " the capitalist class over there, and the united workers over here, why God love me, it would be a million chances to one against the capitalist." (laughter)*
>
> The Rhondda Leader newspaper report, August 1911

In early August 1911 there was increasing pressure on the miners who had been on strike for nine months to settle the dispute. At a huge meeting of over 11,000 miners at the Mid-Rhondda Athletic ground, Captain Tupper, the Seaman's union leader gave a powerful address. He recommended a return to work with dignity, a message which was well received by many in the crowd.

After the Strike
Restart of the Cambrian Collieries

Rush for Working Places

What the Future Holds

Mid-Rhondda woke up on Monday morning with the joyful buzz of the Cambrian Collieries machinery singing in its ears. It was like waking from a torpor, and the community realised that the memorable and disastrous strike had really come to an end. Tradesmen took down the shutters from their shop windows with a strange light in their eyes – eyes that have lacked lustre for many a long day. Visions of renewed prosperity after the unexampled period of stagnation and hopelessness braced their nerves; even the dogs on the streets seemed to impart a new note in their barks, and the tabby cat mewed in the Minor key in the realization that the day of stinted diet was now gone by.

And the workmen going to their employment. The very sound of their hob-nailed boots clattering upon the pavements was the sweetest music that has fallen on the ears for months past. How they strode along, the pockets of their coats bulging outwards with their food-box and water-jack, their arms swinging in rhythmical unison with their steps and faces lit up by a joyousness kindled by the hope that the night of despair being at length over, the sun of human happiness would once more shine upon the hearths and homes. It is a long time since a collier descended into the bowels of the mine with so much sun in his heart

The Rhondda Leader, September 1911

Good-bye to Mid-Rhondda
Make up your minds to
Emigrate! Emigrate!
with the
WHITE STAR, DOMINION, CANADIAN PACIFIC AND AMERICAN S.S. LINES.

EVANS & SHORT
PRINTERS, TONYPANDY,
The local Agents, can book you through
DIRECT FROM THE RHONDDA
TO ANY STATION IN THE WORLD!

See Window Bills and Hoardings for next Sailings, or call at our Office.
Moderate Fares! Unexcelled Accommodation!

A colourful account of the return to work in the Rhondda Leader September 1911. For 3,000 miners there wasn't a job to return to, and a significant number left the district to find work. Another solution could be found in the well publicised adverts encouraging emigration. Recruitment for the armed forces from the Rhondda district was the highest ever during the strike.

For those who had had little confidence in the future of the industry there was always the tempting attraction of a new life across the waters in North America, Canada or to one of the other dominions.

The Rhondda Leader regularly reported in the later months of the strike, farewell parties for strikers leaving for a new life in the United States.

Aftermath The Trial of The Miner's Leaders (November 1911)

CAMBRIAN LEADERS SENTENCED.
Imprisonment for Messrs. Hopla and John.

Resulting from the incidents at the Ely Colliery and at Tonypandy, three men were sentence to imprisonment. A fortnight later, summonses were also issued against two of the men's leaders, William John and John Hopla, again in connection with the riots at Ely Pit. Their trial at Pontypridd on 23rd August was adjourned in the interests of peace as delicate negotiations were proceeding to end the strike. Their trial was eventually held at the Assizes Court at Cardiff in November 1911, several months after the strike had been settled. William John, the Chairman of the Cambrian Workmen's Joint Committee and a deacon of a Baptist Chapel in Tonypandy, together with John Hopla, an Executive Member of the South Wales Miners' Federation, were accused of:

> *"Tumultuously disturbing the peace' and assaulting two police inspectors at the Ely Pit on July 25th, 1911."*

Both men denied the charges. An Ely Colliery official admitted that John made attempts to stop the crowd throwing stones but that he asked in such a low tone of voice that the crowd could not hear him. William John in his defence replied, "Always, I said, I believe the riots would only alienate the sympathy of he public from the workmen" The stone throwing was attributed to boys of 14 – 15 years of age.

Although the evidence against the men appeared circumstantial, there was little doubt from the attitude of the prosecution that a conviction would be made. A police inspector informed the court that John,

> *"has given no end of trouble during the last 12 months – he is recognized as leader of the Cambrian Combine and he is very cunning at it. His meetings are held behind closed doors... my Lord. He gives no end of trouble."*

In spite of pleas from Chapel officials who testified to the men's excellent moral character and the many testimonies from the workmen, both William John and John Hopla were found guilty and given the maximum sentences of 12 months hard labour. The sentences aroused wide indignation across mining communities in South Wales and William 'Mabon' MP and Keir Hardie both raised the matter in the House of Commons. Mabon criticized the judge for not taking note of the jury's recommendation for mercy and the prosecution for presenting many incorrect facts to the judge and to the jury.

William John   *John Hopla*

In April 1912 the jail sentences were later commuted to six months after the then Home secretary McKenna informed the Miners' Federation that due to the absence of disturbance during the recent strike (Minimum wage dispute) and the efforts of the miners to preserve order he thought the occasion was right to show clemency by reducing the sentences on the Rhondda strike leaders.

Both men received a 'hero's welcome' at a mass meeting at Tonypandy. William John went on to become one of Rhondda's Members of Parliament but John Hopla died a year and a half later aged 32.

> *'At the Glamorgan Assizes at Cardiff (Thursday) morning, sentences were delivered on William John (32) and John Hopla (31) checkweighers, Tonypandy. It will be remembered that after a hearing attended over three days, both prisoners who figured prominently as leaders of the recent Cambrian strike, were found guilty of riotous assembling at Penygraig in July last. Both prisoners were sentenced to twelve month's imprisonment with hard labour. Henry Hopla, brother of the prisoner John Hopla who was charged with unlawfully wounding P.C. Ballard of the Worcester police was sentenced to nine months imprisonment with hard labour.'*

Newspaper Report, November 1911.

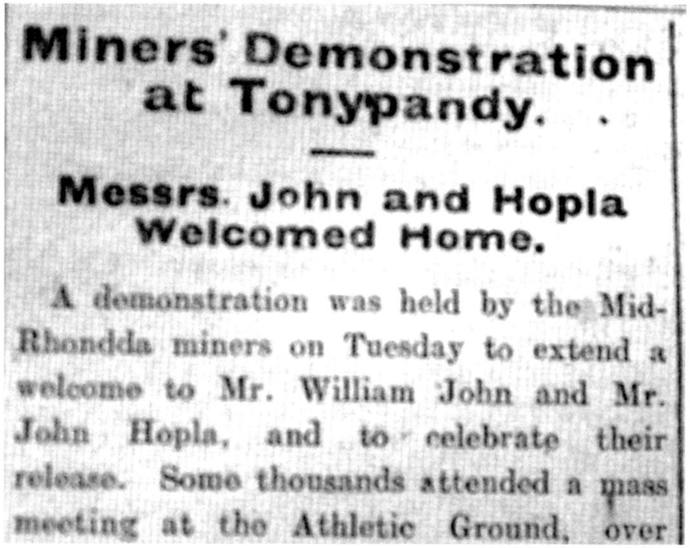

Aftermath Miners' Leaders Homecoming 1912

Miners' Demonstration at Tonypandy.

Messrs. John and Hopla Welcomed Home.

A demonstration was held by the Mid-Rhondda miners on Tuesday to extend a welcome to Mr. William John and Mr. John Hopla, and to celebrate their release. Some thousands attended a mass meeting at the Athletic Ground, over

A plaque to John Hopla, the miners' leader who died in March 1914 aged 32. It was formerly placed on the wall of the Llwynypia Miners' Library and Institute

The crowd at Mid-Rhondda Athletic ground welcome home Will John and John Hopla after their release from prison

The imprisonment of the Rhondda miners' leaders was met with much criticism across the mining communities in South Wales.

The Aftermath

Welcome home to Mid-Rhondda for William John and John Hopla (sitting behind the speaker) having served six months jail sentences

Sixty-four years later... and controversy still rages around the Tonypandy riots. An exhibition on the subject, mounted earlier this month by pupils of the town's grammar school, annoyed author ALEXANDER CORDELL, who saw it as an attempt to diminish Winston Churchill's role in sending in troops, which he described as "a flagrant disregard for truth". The school's head of history, DAVID LENNOX MADDOX, replies...

Flashback to 1910—shops in Tonypandy shuttered and barricaded after the riots.

Why we say Churchill did NOT call in the troops

CHURCHILL WAY

Callaghan accuses Churchill of vendetta

David G. Rosser, Political Editor, writes: The row brought a sequel last night when Mr. Churchill, M.P. for Stretford, wrote to Mr. Callaghan demanding the withdrawal of "no doubt an unintended slur against a not unrespected former holder of your present office who is no longer able to answer for himself."

In his letter Mr. Churchill accused Mr. Callaghan of indulging in a cheap smear against his grandfather when he must have known his charge was wholly without foundation. He said Sir Winston had stopped troops being sent to Tonypandy, had been rebuked in the *Times* of November 9, 1910 for refusing to send troops, and that no miners were shot at Tonypandy.

Churchill, the miners' friend? — Page 12.

● MR. WINSTON CHURCHILL ... accused Mr. Callaghan of indulging in a cheap smear against his grandfather.

155

The Aftermath The Political Impact 1911 - 2010

1911 The Immediate Repercussions

The events were not to be forgotten. The strike saw the end of the old Liberal leadership of the SWMF. William Abrahams 'Mabon', the President of the SWMF was defeated in a ballot for a seat on the Executive Committee of the International Miners' Federation and tendered his resignation as President in 1912. The younger miners whose leadership had been nurtured in the lodges during the strike were confidently taking positions of power in the Federation. Will John, the young Chairman of the Joint Workmen's Committee was within a few years elected as a member of Parliament for the Rhondda.

1926. Winston Churchill changed political parties and in 1926 was Home Secretary in the Conservative government. His role in undermining the 9 day 'General Strike' and the defeat of the miners who remained on strike for 7 months was not forgotten in South Wales valleys,

1945-51 Political Arena 1945-51

In the post 1945 period, the Labour Party had succeeded in forming its first majority government. Winston Churchill, was the Conservative leader of the opposition. His personal popularity arising from his war leadership was high but this was not mirrored in South Wales *"where his activities, real or alleged, during the 1910 Tonypandy riots and the 1926 General Strike, were rooted in popular folklore."*

1949 Churchill Way.

The decision of the Cardiff City Council to honour Churchill by naming a new roadway "Churchill Way", led to outcries from Labour leaders throughout the South Wales Valleys.

1950 Election.

The 'Tonypandy Affair' was considered so contentious that during the bitter election campaign in1950 all Conservative candidates and agents were briefed about the South Wales Miners' Dispute of 1910. The Conservative party issued a circular stating that Churchill *'allowed the troops to be drafted into the area as a reserve to the police, but they were not used.'*

During Churchill's election campaign visit to Cardiff in February 1950 he re-opened the controversy. In his speech at Ninian Park football Ground he told the large crowd that he had not been responsible for the dispatch of the military to Tonypandy in 1910. His role had been initially to hold back the troops and to send Metropolitan policemen instead.

His speech provoked considerable re-action heightened now by the context of the election in which Labour was slipping from power. Labour MPs fired missives to the press offering their interpretations of Churchill's role as Home Secretary 40 years previously. In the Rhondda Valley an election manifesto in 1951 used the issue to galvanise support by asking the electorate to speak for those who fought the fight in 1910. The appearance of Churchill on cinema newsreels in the Valleys was greeted by loud booing and hissing.

1974 Alexander Cordell wrote critically to the press after hearing remarks about Churchill's role in sending in the military made by pupils of the local Tonypandy Grammar school contained in an award winning exhibition.

1978 House of Commons Debate on Miners' Wages

Ironically in 1978, when the Speaker of the House of Commons was the Rt. Hon. George Thomas who was born in 1910, and was "a son" of Tonypandy, the old scars again emerged during a debate about miners' pay. The late Sir Winston Churchill's grandson was taken to task by the Labour Prime Minister, James Callaghan, for certain remarks he had made. Callaghan accused him of "pursuing the vendetta of his family against the miners… at Tonypandy." The remarks caused uproar in the House and for several days radio, television and newspaper columns again attempted to put the historical record straight.

NEW CARDIFF STREET WILL BE CALLED CHURCHILL WAY

CARDIFF'S new highway, running between Queen-street and Bute-terrace and over the culverted dock feeder, has been named Churchill Way as a tribute to the great British war leader.

Western Mail and South Wales News January 1949

In January 1949 Cardiff City Council agreed by 30 votes to 19 to a recommendation by the Lord Mayor that a new highway be named Churchill Way as a tribute to the war leader. An amendment to call the road Pembroke terrace was defeated and a suggestion of 'Attlee Alley' was ignored.

A proposal that the name should be called Heol Churchill was narrowly defeated by 21 votes to 18.

Opposition members felt uncomfortable about naming the road after a political figure. Whilst acknowledging Churchill's war leadership they the raised the matter of Churchill's record before the war and since the war.

One councillor reminded the meeting that 'Tonypandy men had long memories.'

At the time a prospective Conservative candidate for Caerphilly told a meeting that "As a matter of fact, Mr. Churchill was responsible for stopping the troops and not sending them. He sent police ,and the troops were held in reserve."

Chartwell,
Westerham
7th February, 1949

My dear Lord Mayor,

I much regret not having answered your most kind letter earlier. I read with pleasure the newspaper accounts of the debate in the City Council and of the spirited and effective manner in which you defended my claim to the honour of the "Churchill Way."

You send me now a most attractive invitation, which I and my family would gladly accept. I am however so much burdened at the present time that I must beg you to excuse me. I have the most vivid memories of my visit to Cardiff, and your hospitality and consideration.

I have never seen crowds more friendly in any of the numerous cities in which I have been welcomed,

I see that one of the Labour men, referred to Tonypandy as a great crime I had committed in the past. I am having the facts looked up and will write to you again upon the subject. According to my recollections the action I took at Tonypandy was to stop the troops being sent to control the strikers for fear of shooting and I was much attacked by the Conservative opposition for this "weakness", Instead I sent Metropolitan Police who charged with their rolled mackintoshes and no one was hurt. The Metropolitan Police played football with the strikers at the weekend-end.

I will let you know the results of my researches.

I hope you will forgive me for being so tardy in replying and also understand why I cannot comply with your gratifying invitation. I am sending you a copy of my book "Painting as a Pastime", which I have inscribed for you and which I hope you will accept.

Yours sincerely,
Winston S. Churchill

The Right Hon. The Lord Mayor of Cardiff

Winston Churchill's reply to an invitation to visit Cardiff in 1949. He makes reference to the controversy over the naming of Churchill Way

In the bitter election campaign of February 1950 Churchill visited South Wales and addressed a large crowd at Ninian Park, Cardiff. In his speech he re-opened old political wounds by references to his actions as Home Secretary (as a Liberal) some forty years earlier in dealing with the Tonypandy disturbances. Labour members from across South Wales used this as a further opportunity to attack the Prime Minister. Ness Edwards MP for Caerphilly, Parliamentary Secretary to the Ministry of Labour was vitriolic in his condemnation of Churchill's earlier role. In the Rhondda, the local Labour candidate made the issue the focal point of his election manifesto.

The Election Manifesto distributed in Tonypandy in 1950 by Labour candidate

RHONDDA WEST CONSTITUENCY MANIFESTO

Troops in Tonypandy.
What is Tonypandy's Reply to Churchill's Ninian Park Speech?
Why did Churchill refer to Tonypandy at all? Nobody heckled him.

Nobody provoked him. WAS IT HIS CONSCIENCE THAT PROMPTED HIM TO MENTION TONYPANDY? He was only 20 miles away. He might have heard the echos of the tramping feet of the men who marched through Tonypandy and Clydach Vale during those bitter months of conflict.

The voters of Tonypandy and Clydach Vale have to give their answer to Churchill on the 23rd February. SPEAK FOR YOURSELF – SPEAK FOR THOSE WHO FOUGHT THE FIGHT IN 1910 BUT WHO HAS SINCE PASSED OUT OF HIS LIFE. ANSWER FOR THEM. Let Churchill know that you remember 1910 and the part HE played in requesting the use of the military forces.

THE MAXIMUM POLL FOR THE LABOUR CANDIDATE IS THE ONLY EFFECTIVE ANSWER TO CHURCHILL'S NINIAN PARK SPEECH.
-USE YOUR VOTE
DON'T BE A POLITICAL SLACKER
RALLY TO THE POLL AND GIVE LABOUR A RECORD MAJORITY
VOTE FOR THE LABOUR CANDIDATE
IORWERTH R. THOMAS

GENERAL ELECTION 1950
Ness Edward's response to Churchill's Ninian Park speech
Reported in the 'Daily Herald' 10 February 1950

THE TONYPANDY TROOPS
Ness Edwards answers Churchill.
Statements made by Mr. Churchill in his speech at Cardiff on Wednesday were directly challenged last night by Mr. Ness Edwards, Parliamentary Secretary, Ministry of Labour, in the Caerphilly Division of Glamorgan.
'The miners are so infuriated," he said. "that Mr. Churchill has inflicted a fatal blow to Tory aspirations in the South Wales coalfield." Mr. Churchill in his speech, giving what he called "the true story of Tonypandy," said he stopped the movement of troops to the area and sent 850 Metropolitan Police with the sole object of preventing loss of life. The troops were kept in the background and all the contact made with the rioters was by unarmed London Police, who charged with rolled-up mackintoshes.

Mr. Ness Edwards said last night: "Mr. Churchill describes as a 'cruel lie' the allegations that he used troops against the miners at Tonypandy in 1910. In addition to his other virtues Mr. Churchill must have a convenient memory. "What virtue Mr. Churchill may claim out of the incident is due to the fact that he issued orders for the troops to move and detained some of them on November 9 for one night at Swindon. On November 10, these troops entrained for Pontypridd where General Macready, the commanding officer set up his headquarters at the New Inn."'
(Later Commissioner of the Metropolitan Police and Commander of British Forces in Ireland)

Mr. Edwards quoted the following excerpts from General Macready's book.
'In order to counter these tactics (of the strikers) small bodies of infantry on the higher ground, keeping level with the police on the main road, moved slowly down the side tracks and by a little gentle persuasion with the bayonet drove the stone throwers into the arms of the police on the lower road.'

Mr. Edwards added: *"These are the facts, recorded not by a romantic politician, but by the Tory newspaper at the time, and by the Commanding Officer of the forces employed. Mr. Churchill did use the military against the miners at Tonypandy, and the miners will never forget it."*

The Aftermath **1950 The Election Campaign**

Winston Churchill addresses a large crowd at Ninian Park, Cardiff, during the election campaign 1950

The Aftermath 1974 Alexander Cordell Gives His Opinion

You can't absolve Churchill

I SEE that pupils in a South Wales school have been researching into the Tonypandy Riots.

During an interview it was enlisted that new light had been thrown on the Tonypandy affair of 1911 in that Churchill, the then Home Secretary, was not responsible for the bringing in of troops.

Further, it was stated that the "old people" of the valleys have apparently been wrong all these years: that Churchill was not guilty of the accusation.

I think it is laudable that the younger generation (led by their teacher) should show such interest in their history, for it is upon the deeds of the past that the future is forged. But I cannot allow to pass such a flagrant disregard for truth.

Let us show new light on history, by all means, but let a new countenance glow with historical fact.

A telegram to the Chief Constable of Glamorgan, by Churchill (Tuesday, November 8, 1910) states: "As it appears from telephone messages just received that the situation has become more serious Home Secretary has authorised Gen. Macready, if you desire it, to move all cavalry into the disturbed district without delay. You may communicate this to Gen. Macready in case Home Secretary's telegram has not reached him . . ."

A little later Keir Hardy complained in Parliament: "The military have been called out in connection with this dispute in South Wales, not only without any grave necessity, but without any necessity at all . . ."

Old photographs tell us that the troops were actually present in Tonypandy. The fact that the soldiers behaved in an orderly manner, led by a very reasonable officer — that brutality on the part of officialdom came largely from the Metropolitan Police (and the strikers themselves) — in no way lifts responsibility from Churchill in calling in the military.

Had shooting started (as happened earlier at Featherstone in Yorkshire, where colliers were shot down) Churchill, and only Churchill could have been held to blame.

So go slowly, lads — I'm full of admiration for both you and your teacher — but take it slowly.

This is how we learn of history — by digging out the facts and examining them in debate. The fact that we are able to discuss this openly today is probably because of the war courage of Winston Churchill (still the greatest enemy of the working class this century has known).

But this doesn't mean you can give him a lift now things are not going so well in his favour.

The old people are right, you know — they always are. Whether you like it or not — the old man, after delaying them, sent troops in. The facts of it speak more loudly today than the batons on the skulls of Tonypandy Square.

ALEXANDER CORDELL.
Waen Wen,
near Bangor.

In 1974 Alexander Cordell wrote to the South Wales Echo complaining about the interpretation pupils at Tonypandy Grammar School had made about the role of Winston Churchill in sending in the troops to the valleys in 1910. The Echo's Postbag received responses for several days afterwards.

What would you have done, Mr. Cordell?

WITH regard to Alexander Cordell's recent letter, Churchill was never the enemy of the working class. He was their champion.

Unfortunately, people like Mr. Cordell are always ready to remember any flaw in a good man. But what would he have done in the same circumstances?

It is easy to criticise, but when statesmen are elected by the people they have to make decisions, whether popular or not.

Thank God the people of this country chose him for their leader, otherwise our life might now be very different.

I therefore absolve Churchill and say well done. His name will live for evermore.

A. F. UPHILL.
Plymouth Wood Road,
Ely,
Cardiff.

★

THE Tonypandy Riots demanded a man of action. World War II demanded a man of action. Churchill was that man.

I suggest that Mr. Cordell should stick to fiction.

J. C. WALKER.
Smith End,
Barley,
Herts.

★

NOVELIST Alexander Cordell seems shocked and dismayed that an unprejudiced class of youthful researchers, under the supervision of an experienced teacher, have exonerated Winston Churchill from the charge that he sent troops to the Tonypandy Riots in 1911.

The indignant Mr. Cordell seems to think it is nothing short of sacrilege to destroy a legend that has been nursed and cherished in the Rhondda for two generations.

When we recall that tens of millions of persons died in the two World Wars, with millions more permanently disabled, it is obvious that the commonplace local incident at Tonypandy has been blown up and exaggerated to grotesque and ridiculous proportions.

In any case even if Churchill sent troops to the riots he was only doing his duty. What else could he have done?

Who does Mr. Cordell think will believe his ludicrous statement that Churchill was the greatest enemy of the working class this century has known. If he does a little more research he will discover that around the same period as the Tonypandy affair, Churchill was backing and assisting Lloyd George to get the old age pension, health insurance and employment exchange acts on the Statute Book.

W. H. PRICE.
Fidlas Avenue,
Llanishen, Cardiff.

STRIKES PLEDGE

NEW Year resolutions will soon fill our minds. Here's a thought:
If working men and

Western Mail Report on the debate 30th November, 1978

RETRACT SLUR ON WAR LEADER, SAY TORIES

Callaghan accuses Churchill of vendetta

By JOHN DEANS

MR. CALLAGHAN sparked a Commons row last night when he accused Sir Winston Churchill of maintaining a vendetta against the miners.

It all started when the wartime leader's grandson, M.P. Mr. Winston Churchill, asked what action would be taken against the miners because only one-tenth of their 36.5 per cent. pay award had been recouped in increased productivity.

It ended with angry exchanges between Labour and Tory M.P.s and demands that Mr. Callaghan withdrew his remarks.

Mr. Callaghan asked Mr. Churchill not to pursue his family's vendetta against the miners—thought to be a reference to Sir Winston's action as Home Secretary during the Tonypandy Riots in South Wales in 1910 and later during the General Strike in 1926.

Mr. Churchill, backed by chanting Tories, later demanded a withdrawal from the Premier

Deputy Tory leader Mr. Willie Whitelaw stepped in and called on Mr. Callaghan to "withdraw that cheap and totally unnecessary slur."

But the Prime Minister replied, "The action of Sir Winston over Tonypandy is a matter of historical dispute. I take one side and you take the other in this quarrel. I can tell you what we felt in South Wales and all I say to Mr. Churchill is that I hope he won't pursue the vendetta against the miners."

David G. Rosser, Political Editor, writes: The row brought a sequel last night when Mr. Churchill, M.P. for Stretford, wrote to Mr. Callaghan demanding the withdrawal of "no doubt an unintended slur against a not unrespected former holder of your present office who is no longer able to answer for himself."

In his letter Mr. Churchill accused Mr. Callaghan of indulging in a cheap smear against his grandfather when he must have known his charge was wholly without foundation. He said Sir Winston had stopped troops being sent to Tonypandy, had been rebuked in the *Times* of November 9, 1910 for refusing to send troops, and that no miners were shot at Tonypandy.

Churchill, the miners' friend? — Page 12.

● MR. WINSTON CHURCHILL . . . accused Mr. Callaghan of indulging in a cheap smear against his grandfather.

'Sixty eight years of history erupted in the Commons yesterday by the Prime Minister which left M.P.'s on opposite sides almost snarling at each other. The issue was: did Winston Churchill when Home Secretary send soldiers to Tonypandy to put down the Miners' unrest? Or was he the one who stopped them and replaced them with police? Mr. Callaghan triggered it off when he wound up a reply to Mr. Winston Churchill on miners' pay demands with the riposte, "I hope you are not going to pursue the vendetta of your family against the miners".'
Western Mail, 1978

HOUSE OF COMMONS OFFICIAL REPORT PARLIAMENTARY DEBATES (HANSARD)

Mr. Churchill: The Prime Minister has spoken of the importance of productivity deals. Will he say what steps he and his Administration are taking to monitor existing productivity deals, and in particular in the case of the miners? As the Prime Minister well knows, this year the miners received a 36.5 per cent pay increase. Will he explain what action he proposes to take in the light of the fact that less than one- tenth of that sum has been earned in increased productivity?

The Prime Minister: I do not propose to go into this matter myself. If the hon. Gentleman has any questions to put to my right hon. Friend and Secretary of State for Energy, no doubt he will do so. I hope that the hon. Gentleman will not pursue the vendetta of his family against the miners – (Interruption) – at Tonypandy for the third generation.

Mr. Churchill: Mr. Speaker, would it be in order for the Prime Minister to withdraw his wholly false smear accusation against my late grandfather, whose vendetta was against not the miners, but the Nazis?

The Prime Minister: The actions of the late Sir Winston Churchill in Tonypandy are a matter of historical dispute. I take one side of the quarrel. It may be that the right hon. Gentleman takes another side of that quarrel. I can only tell him what we in South Wales feel about the actions that were taken on that occasion.

I hope that the hon. Member of the Stretford (Mr. Churchill) will not pursue a vendetta against the miners.

Mr. Churchill: Further to that point of order, Mr. Speaker. The Prime Minister is seeking to advance a hoary old chestnut of Socialism by seeking to suggest that the late Sir Winston Churchill sent troops to Tonypandy when the right hon. Gentleman should very well known that it was Sir Winston Churchill who detrained them at Didcot and sent instead policemen from the Metropolis. It was completely unjustifiable for the right hon. Gentleman to suggest that the late Sir Winston Churchill sent troops, which was the implication behind his remarks.

The Prime Minister: If I had thought that the remark was untruthful, I would not have made it. The record of the late Sir Winston Churchill in that dispute is a matter which is and continues to be deeply felt in South Wales. (Interruption).

There is no need for Opposition Members to try to make up to the Hon. Member for Stretford for having voted against him in the Defence Committee.

As regards Sir Winston Churchill's record, there is no need for me to add my words to what I am known to feel about him or his service to the country. That is well known. I have said it myself on previous occasions and I have no hesitation in saying it again. However, there is a particular issue here which is unresolved at the bar of history, even now.

Mr. Speaker: Order. This is pursuing the argument. I suggest to the House that we leave the matter. I never thought that the day would come when a pupil of Tonypandy Grammar School would have the last word between both sides of this place on such a matter. I believe that it is to the mutual advantage of this House to leave the matter there.

*Extract from Hansard
30th November 1978*

Protagonists: Labour Prime Minister, James Callaghan, MP for a Cardiff constituency; Conservative MP, Mr Winston Churchill, grandson of Sir Winston Churchill. Chairing proceedings: The Rt. Hon. George Thomas, Speaker of The House of Commons.

THE TIMES

New Printing House Square, London, WC1X 8EZ. Telephone: 01-837 1234

Churchill and Tonypandy

From Sir John Walley

Sir, Seemingly, nothing will stop malevolents among the populations of the South Wales mining valleys pursuing Churchill, even beyond the grave, so long as they can pursuade the ignorant and the gullible that, in 1910, he sent troops to crush the Tonypandy rioters. I was, however, shocked to find in your columns on September 21 an article from Tim Jones which showed no doubt about the truth of this vicious political canard. Calling Churchill's action an "historical blunder", it even went on to give it as a valid explanation for the reluctance of the electors in the Valleys to vote Conservative! Yet the facts about Tonypandy have always been as available to the seeker after truth as the history of Churchill's party political affiliations.

Churchill was, in November, 1910, Asquith's Home Secretary in our last Liberal Party Government and had, among many other things, demonstrated his radical sympathy with Labour by taking the recent President of the TUC into that Ministry as its Industrial Adviser. In a grave local situation, arising from a trade dispute but which ended in mobs looting the inoffensive shopkeepers of Tonypandy, the Chief Constable of Glamorgan made a direct (and successful) appeal to the GOC (Southern Command) for troops and, because of the apparent urgency, these began to move in anticipation of covering Ministerial authority. Immediately Churchill was told of this, he got the Minister of War, Haldane, to halt the infantry units at Swindon and the Cavalry at Cardiff; he then got the Chief Constable to accept, instead, a large contingent of experienced Metropolitan Policemen by special train. None of the troops even saw Tonypandy!

In a leader on November 9, 1910, your predecessor severely attacked Churchill for "interfering with the arrangements demanded by the Chief Constable" and warned him that "if loss of life occurs, which we fear is more than possible, the responsibility will lie with the Home Secretary. The conciliatory message which he sent yesterday to the miners is well meant, of course, but it shows a very inadequate grasp of the situation, and the somewhat maudlin tone in which it is couched is more likely to excite ridicule than respect." With greater percipience, the Editor of *The Manchester Guardian* wrote next day " Mr Churchill was violently attacked in yesterday's *Times* for a decision which in all probability saved many lives. It needed some courage after the Chief Constable had asked for troops to stop the troops when they were on their way and to send policemen instead. But, as usual, the brave course was also the wise one." These quotes are from the second volume of the Churchill Official biography, pages 373-378.

With what I have always felt to be over-optimism, Coventry Patmore once wrote :

The truth is great and shall prevail, When none cares whether it prevail or not.

I hope that, after nearly 68 years, you will allow it to prevail—at least for Churchill's good name with your present readers.

Yours faithfully,
JOHN WALLEY,
46 Rotherwick Road, NW11

Churchill and Tonypandy

From Professor Ronald Frankenberg

Sir, Sir John Walley is alas in error (in his letter published on October 3) concerning Churchill and Tonypandy. Having held the Cavalry in Cardiff by a telegram at 1.30 pm on Tuesday, November 8, 1910, and having sent a public message to the miners; feeling that the situation had worsened at 8 pm the same day he changed his mind and telegraphed both General Macready and the Chief Constable to use the Cavalry if they saw fit.

This news apparently did not reach either the critical leader writer of *The Times* on the 9th nor the supportive leader writer of *The Manchester Guardian* on the 10th Macready did not use the permission until nearly a fortnight later (November 21) when he deployed units of the Lancashire Fusiliers, The Royal Munster Fusiliers, The Devon Regiment and a squadron of Hussars at Penygraig. (The last were in the event delayed by frosty roads.)

A full and fair account of Churcill's actions and the pressures upon him before and after will be found in Robin Page Arnot's *South Wales Miners*. (Allen and Unwin. 1967. pp. 183-218.)

If Churchill remains unpopular in the valleys, it may well be memories of heads broken by the Metropolitan Police which he did send, rather than those of the troops which, temporarily, he held back. I can think of simpler hypotheses for possible persistent dislike of the Conservative Party. Perhaps I can answer both Sir John's quotation from Coventry Patmore and the implications of Josephine Tey's similarly erroneous book, *The Daughter of Time* with this from Edwin Teale:

" You can prove almost anything with the evidence of a small enough segment of time. How often, in any search for truth, the answer of the minute is positive, the answer of the hour qualified, the answers of the year contradictory."

Yours faithfully,
RONALD FRANKENBERG,
Sometime Education Officer,
NUM (South Wales),
Department of Sociology and Social Anthropology,
Keele,
Staffordshire.
October 3.

1978. Part of the correspondence in the press provoked by the clash in Parliament between Prime Minister James Callaghan and Conservative MP, Mr Winston Churchill.

Bibliography

R. Page Arnot	*The Miners "Years of Struggle"* (George Allen and Unwit, Ltd. 1953)
R. Page Arnot	*South Wales Miners 1898-1914* (George Allen and Unwit Ltd. 1967)
Randolph S Churchill	*Winston Churchill – Young Statesman 1901 – 1914* (Heinemann 1967)
Major-General Sir Wyndam Childs	*Episodes and Reflections* (Cassell and Co. Ltd London 1930)
David Evans	*Labour Strife in the South Wales Coalfield 1910-1911* (Educational Publishing Co. Ltd. Cardiff)
Gwyn Evans and David Maddox	*The Tonypandy Riots* (Publ. Mid Glamorgan County Council 1990)
Gwyn Evans and David Maddox	*The Cambrian Combine Strike* Resources Pack (2010)
Bill Jones and Beth Thomas	*Coal's Domain* (National Museum of Wales, 1993)
Gareth Elwyn Jones	*People, Protest and Politics* Case Studies in Twentieth Century Wales (Gomer Press 1987)
T. Herbert and Gareth E. Jones (editors)	*Wales 1880-1914* University of Wales Press (1988)
E.D. Lewis	*The Rhondda Valleys* (Phoenix House London 1959)
Sir Nevil Macready	*Annals of an Active life Vol.1* (Hutchinson 1924)
K.O. Morgan	*Rebirth of a Nation: Wales 1880- 1980* (Oxford University Press 1982)
Ness Edwards	*History of the South Wales Miners' Federation* Vol. 1 (Lawrence and Wishart: London 1938)
Dai Smith	*Wales! Wales?* (George Allen and Unwin 1984)
Dai Smith	*'Tonypandy 1910 – Definitions of Community' Past and Present* (May 1980)
Dai Smith	*Wales A Question for History* (Seren 1999)
L.J. Williams	*'The Road to Tonypandy' Llafur. Vol 1 No. 2* (1973)
HMSO	*Report on the Colliery Disturbances in South Wales* November 1910 (London H.M.S.O. 1911)
Glamorgan Record Office	*Newspaper Files* Glamorgan Record Office, Cardiff
Public Record Office	*Correspondence* between Home Office and Police and Military Authorities
Rhondda CB Library Service	*Rhondda Leader* 1908-1912
Rhondda CB Library Service	*Rhondda Leader* 1905-1912 , *Glamorgan Free Press* 1910-1912, *Pontypridd Observer* 1910-11
Cardiff Central Library	*Various newspaper articles* 1910-11 *Glamorgan Gazette*